REFLECTIONS ON SILVER RIVER

BOOKS AND TRANSLATIONS BY KEN MCLEOD

Reflections on Silver River (2013)

An Arrow to the Heart (2007)

Wake Up to Your Life (2001)

The Great Path of Awakening (1987)

Reflections on Silver River

Tokmé Zongpo's *Thirty-Seven Practices of a Bodhisattva*

translation and commentary by

Ken McLeod

Unfettered Mind Media

Pragmatic Buddhism

Los Angeles

ISBN 978-0-98951-530-6 (hardcover)

ISBN 978-0-98951-531-3 (softcover)

Unfettered Mind Media
www.unfetteredmind.org

Printed in the United States of America
Cover photo: Ebrahim Faraji Tark
Book design: VJB/Scribe

3 5 8 7 9 8 6 4 2

Morning comes whether you set the alarm or not.

—URSULA K. LE GUIN

CONTENTS

If it is better for me to be ill,
Give me the energy to be ill.
If it is better for me to recover,
Give me the energy to recover.
If it is better for me to die,
Give me the energy to die.

SUCH WAS MY FIRST ENCOUNTER WITH TOKMÉ
Zongpo of Silver River (Tib. *rngul-chu thogs-med bzang-po*). I had
been asked to translate *The Great Path of Awakening*, Jamgön Kongtrül's commentary on *Mind Training in Seven Points*. Kongtrül had
included this prayer as a supplement to the instruction "Let go of
hope and fear." It was the strangest prayer I had ever seen and it
made no sense to me. Why would you pray to be ill? Why would
you pray to die? There was no attribution (a common practice in
Tibetan religious literature). I did not know where the prayer came
from or who had written it. In the end, I just translated it as part
of the text and did not think about it any further.

My next encounter was during my first three-year retreat in
France. Our retreat director gave us copies of Tokmé Zongpo's
*Thirty-Seven Practices of a Bodhisattva (Tib. rgyal-sras lag-len so-bdun-
ma)* and suggested we study it. It was clearly a text of the *lam-rim*
genre—a sequential presentation of the Mahayana path as it was
understood and practiced in the Tibetan tradition. Most texts of
this genre run to hundreds of pages and cover largely the same
material in greater or lesser detail, depending on the author. From
my point of view, the only thing *Thirty-Seven Practices* had going
for it was that it was mercifully short, a summary that covered the
whole path in just thirty-seven verses.

In that retreat, I studied many different texts, gradually

putting together the intricate baroque mosaic of Tibetan Buddhism. Tokmé Zongpo's name kept cropping up in odd places. Even though this person had clearly exerted considerable influence over the centuries, I was too caught up in my own challenges to pay much attention to yet another medieval scholar who had written yet another text about the bodhisattva path.

The intensity of practice in the retreat brought up deep-seated blocks that broke me physically and emotionally. Often I was too ill to do the assigned practices. Nothing I read helped, nor did any of the advice I received from my teacher or our retreat director. All I could do was endure the physical pain and emotional misery as best I could. I tried, without much success, to keep my mind from running amok. Not knowing what else to do, I turned to taking and sending (Tibetan *gtong len*, pron. tonglen), a practice I knew well. In Kongtrül's commentary, the text I had translated before the retreat, I came across that strange prayer again:

If it is better for me to be ill,
Give me the energy to be ill.
If it is better for me to recover,
Give me the energy to recover.
If it is better for me to die,
Give me the energy to die.

Now it spoke to me. Physically I was beyond miserable and emotionally I was in even worse shape. I was afraid, too, because I did not see how I could go on. I kept hoping for a way out—something, anything, that would dispel the pain and depression.

The prayer did not alleviate my physical or emotional distress. I just said it again and again, struggling to accept what was happening in me. I continued the practice of taking and sending because it is a practice you can do even when you are extremely ill or upset or both. Then something happened. To this day I am not sure what changed, but I do know that I gave up on my life. I gave up any hope that I would ever be happy or well again or I would ever be enlightened or awake or whatever you want to call it. Those possibilities were so utterly remote as to be nonexistent.

One spring day I stumbled out of my room for some fresh air. I could barely stand and had to lean against a tree for support. The acacia trees were in flower, white blossoms against a clear blue sky. The warmth of the sun dispelled the consistent chill of our cinder-block cells. As I looked around, I felt quiet in the joy of the moment and at peace in the pain. Then it hit me. This was the point of practice—nothing more! Life presents you with different experiences. Every experience has infinite dimensions. Can you experience all of them without struggling against any of them? If you can, then suffering comes to an end—so obvious, so simple, so deep, and so wonderful.

Even after the retreat, my struggles were far from over. I returned to this prayer again and again. Eventually, much to my surprise, I learned that Tokmé Zongpo had written it when faced with a long, unrelenting and debilitating illness. The same prayer that had addressed the travails of a fourteenth century monk also spoke to me. Tokmé Zongpo, it seemed, understood the human condition very deeply. I started to appreciate that he was more than just another medieval scholar. He knew how to accept all that life offered, the good and the bad, and not lose his humanity.

Born in 1295 in Central Tibet, Tokmé Zongpo was orphaned at an early age. His mother died when he was three, his father two years later. His grandmother then looked after him. When she died four years later, an uncle took him in. From his uncle, he learned how to read and write (a rare accomplishment for an ordinary Tibetan in the fourteenth century). Encouraged by his uncle, he entered monastic life at the age of fourteen. From these humble beginnings, Tokmé Zongpo emerged to become a prodigious scholar, a respected abbot, a devoted practitioner, and an icon of compassion.

While a young monk in the Kadampa tradition, Tokmé Zongpo quickly mastered the classical curriculum. By the time he was nineteen, he was being hailed as a second Asanga, his namesake, the great fourth century Indian master (Tokmé is the Tibetan for Asanga).

Life in a Tibetan monastery in the fourteenth century was far from easy. While monasteries usually provided food and shelter, for all other expenses—from basic personal needs to offerings for training and teaching—a monk depended on relatives, patronage, or the performance of rituals and empowerments to attract offerings. Tokmé Zongpo had no relatives and his humble and quiet manner did not attract patrons. When he had difficulty in making ends meet, he was advised to perform rituals for the villagers or give empowerments. Such a materialistic approach—using spiritual ceremonies for financial gain—was unthinkable to him. Instead, he sat down and wrote a poem to remind himself of the essential practices of his chosen path. That poem comes down to us today as *Thirty-Seven Practices of a Bodhisattva*.

When he was thirty-two, Tokmé Zongpo was appointed abbot of a monastery. Nine years later, he refused a subsequent appointment, insisting that a better person be found. Retiring to a hermitage in Ngülchu (Silver River), he devoted himself to practice for the next twenty years. Instances of his compassion became legend in Tibet. Beggars refused to take alms from him because they knew he would give them his last cup of barley flour or the robe off his back. Soldiers stopped their attacks when he was present. Wolves and sheep played peacefully together in front of him.

Many years later when I was living in Los Angeles, I went to hear Garchen Rinpoche teach. Here was a person who knew what it was to suffer on a level very different from the challenges I had faced in retreat. He had spent years in a Chinese prison in the harshest conditions—hard labor, rags for clothes, unspeakable food. One of the most respected dzogchen teachers of the twentieth century was in the same prison. Garchen Rinpoche was able to study with him, even though prisoners were not allowed to talk with each other. Practice reports and practice guidance consisted of one-sentence or one-word grunts as they passed each other in the hallways. Today Garchen Rinpoche radiates a peace and compassion that can come only from deep understanding and experience. He hands out copies of *Thirty-Seven Practices* to everyone who comes to hear him teach. It is a text he treasures above all others. Clearly I had missed something.

I downloaded a copy of the text in Tibetan and read it carefully. This time I appreciated Tokmé Zongpo in quite a different way. His language was clear and his advice uncompromising.

Sensual pleasures are like salty water:
The deeper you drink, the thirstier you become.
Any object you attach to,
Right away, let it go—this is the practice of a bodhisattva.

Tokmé Zongpo does not present lengthy utilitarian arguments about the undesirability of desire. He simply states what all of us know but conveniently forget. Patterns associated with pleasure are insidious: we always want more. He does not say, "Don't enjoy things." He just says, "Let it go." This advice is as relevant for a bar of chocolate as it is for the bliss in meditation practice. Both experiences can trap us.

In another verse, he writes:

Even if someone humiliates you and denounces you
In front of a crowd of people,
Think of this person as your teacher
And humbly honor him—this is the practice of a bodhisattva.

Shame is a very powerful emotion. Can you imagine being publicly shamed, being able to bear it patiently, and, in that moment, appreciating the person who humiliates you for putting you viscerally in touch with your illusory sense of self, and then honoring him or her? By putting the matter in such uncompromising language, Tokmé Zongpo lays down a challenge: can you experience whatever life throws at you without reacting? If his life is any indication, Tokmé Zongpo took his own advice seriously. Most of us, if we do not feel a stab of terror deep in our guts when we read this verse, just shake our heads and laugh a little sheepishly.

Thirty-Seven Practices is about the bodhisattva path. What, then, is a bodhisattva? One answer is that a bodhisattva is a person who lives and breathes compassion. Compassion is ordinarily understood as an emotion, but the compassion of a bodhisattva is not a sentiment. It is not pity. It is a quality of awareness itself, the knowing that is the core of our humanity. Most of us have had experiences of this kind of compassion, moments when mind and heart are crystal clear, and we just respond to the needs of the moment.

Such experiences often arise when a friend or family member is faced with a great loss—the death of a child, the end of a relationship, a natural disaster that destroys a home or a life. In such moments we are right there with our friend. We may sit in silence with her, but it is the silence of connection. When we speak, we do not know where the words come from, but they come. In retrospect we remember such moments as moments of magical intimacy, an intimacy in which we are completely with the other person, with a compassion that knows the pain yet is free from any pity, judgment, sentimentality or despair. In such moments, we don't have a sense of "I" and "other." We are just there, completely aware and present.

A person might be said to be awake when he or she can move into this awareness, this way of experiencing life, at will. The word *bodhi* means "awakening" and *sattva* means "being." Thus, a bodhisattva is a person who is or aspires to be awake. When this awareness is present, you simply respond to the pain and struggles of others in whatever way is possible in your life. In other words, a bodhisattva lives and breathes compassion.

This is an ideal, of course, and, like any ideal, it is impossible to achieve. Inevitably we fail, and we fail over and over again. Through those repeated efforts, however, we forge a path in life, a path that leads to a profound acceptance of the human condition. The point here is that, in striving for an ideal, we inevitably run into our own limitations. The real challenges we face in life are in our limitations, and through those, we find our way. As Suzuki Roshi taught in *Zen Mind, Beginner's Mind*:

> In your very imperfections you will find the basis for your firm, way-seeking mind.

With that acceptance comes an understanding of the dignity of what it means to be human. That understanding takes expression as an equally profound appreciation of life itself. Leo Strauss, one of the leading philosophers of the twentieth century, writes:

> By becoming aware of the dignity of mind, we realize the true ground of the dignity of man and therewith the goodness of the world, whether we understand it as created or uncreated, which is the home of man because it is the home of the human mind.

The way of a bodhisattva is a way of internal clarity, a clarity that expresses itself in compassion and enables us to bring all our skills and capabilities to the challenges life presents. When we have the capacity to experience whatever life brings to us, we are not thrown into turmoil by our own reactions. If we can experience the joys, tribulations and pain of life without being carried away by them and without suppressing them, then we are free, or as free as is possible within the human condition.

What is this freedom? Most people think of freedom as freedom to act as they wish or as freedom from unpleasantness, obligation or responsibility. These are infantile notions of freedom that are based on the desire to control what we experience. The illusion of control is itself an indication of a lack of freedom. As long as we are human, we are never free to do whatever we want. Nor will we ever be free from pain and unpleasantness. The bodhisattva's freedom is not about "freedom to" or "freedom from." It is not about understanding life and being able to control it. It is a freedom that comes when we accept that life is just life. Only then can we be truly responsive to the pain and struggles of others.

In *Thirty-Seven Practices*, Tokmé Zongpo sets out his own path, a path that consists of thirty-seven points through which he seeks to develop the skills and capacities to meet the challenges that life presents without struggling against them. Uncompromising in their disregard for conventional notions of success and failure, these verses often leave the modern reader feeling inadequate, unable to imagine how anyone could take such an approach to life. Tokmé Zongpo wrote these verses for himself, as reminders to reach beyond his own conditioned sense of the possible. Despite his extraordinary example, he probably felt as inadequate as you or I.

The text itself follows classical forms. Tokmé Zongpo opens with a traditional Sanskrit invocation to Lokeshvara, the deity or mythic figure who embodied the ideal of awakened compassion in the Buddhism of medieval India. In the introductory verses he pays homage to Lokeshvara and his own teachers and sets out his intention for this poem. The next thirty-seven verses describe the key points of a bodhisattva's practice. In the concluding section he follows a traditional formula: a restatement of intention, a request for tolerance of any errors and his own dedication.

Today many people practice meditation and pursue Buddhism with the idea that it will make them better people, more effective in their work or more successful in life. Tokmé Zongpo would have found such a utilitarian approach incomprehensible. The spiritual practice described here is not about becoming a better person. It is not about increasing your skills, being more effective in your life, healing old wounds or being successful. It is about finding a way that leaves you at peace in your life and free to respond to others in whatever way is appropriate.

As your practice matures and deepens, old wounds may come to the surface and heal. You may well become more effective and more responsive in your interactions with others. However, these are side effects of spiritual practice. When you take them as the aim of practice, you reduce practice to a form of self-improvement. The focus on yourself separates you from life, and you limit the chances of your finding a way to embrace the perplexing and baffling mystery of the human condition.

Tokmé Zongpo's instructions here and the example of his own life paint a very different picture. In reading these verses, we can feel how he is talking to himself as much as others. He did not seek fame or fortune. He left a life of security and respect as an abbot and spent most of his life practicing in retreat. Even though he is regarded as an exemplar of compassion in the Tibetan tradition of Buddhism, he likely felt that he had not achieved his ideal and continued to deepen his understanding, quietly and humbly.

The first nine verses set out the discipline and practices that establish a foundation for spiritual growth. Appreciate this opportunity, he advises, and be prepared to make significant changes in your life, internally if not externally. Do not feel that you have to change the form of your life. More important is to change how you approach life and how you live it. To support those changes, create conditions in your life that free you from chaos and confusion.

> Don't engage disturbances and emotional reactions
>   gradually fade away;
> Don't engage distractions and spiritual practice
>   naturally grows;
> Keep awareness clear and vivid and confidence in the
>   way arises.
> Rely on silence—this is the practice of a bodhisattva.

Pick your friends and associates carefully, as they will affect you deeply, for better or worse. Do not rely on what others deem important. Set your aspirations high and do your best.

The next section, verses ten to eighteen, introduces taking and sending, the practice on which Tokmé Zongpo relied. In taking and sending meditation, you imagine taking on the suffering of others and sending them your own good fortune:

Therefore, exchange completely your happiness
For the suffering of others—this is the practice of
a bodhisattva.

At first glance this is a preposterous idea, particularly in this day and age when we have been heavily conditioned to regard our own happiness, whether material, emotional or spiritual, to be the purpose of life. We are unable to tolerate the emotional sensations—anger, jealousy, shame, grief, fear and many others—that arise when our happiness or well-being is compromised. In taking and sending practice, we magnify by many times the intensity of these emotional sensations by imagining that we are taking on the struggles of others and giving away our own happiness and joy. In effect, we are rubbing two sticks together. One stick is our habituated self-centeredness. The other is the other-centeredness of taking and sending. Eventually, both sticks catch fire and burn up and we are left groundless, clear and responsive, free from attachment to any center.

Consider this practice in the light of the three questions posed by the sage Hillel the Elder:

If I'm not for myself, who will be?
If I'm only for myself, what am I?
If not now, when?

We cannot ignore that we are alone in this life. Nor can we ignore that a life without relationships is not a life—not a human life, anyway. Nor can we ignore that we never know how much time we have to change our relationship with life. It is not hard to imagine that neither time nor culture would have prevented this ancient Jewish scholar and this medieval Tibetan monk from understanding each other.

All of us have encountered circumstances in which we have been wronged, in which people have treated us unkindly or inflicted harm on us, with or without justification. In verses twelve to eighteen, Tokmé Zongpo sets out how he aspires to be in such situations. He puts us directly in touch with the raw feelings that arise: violation, anger, disbelief, shame and fear. These are very powerful feelings, and we usually react in anger, seeing the person who attacked us as an enemy and seeking some form of retribution. In verse twelve, he poses the situation of someone stealing everything we own. Rarely does someone steal everything we own, but whether someone steals a small item or a treasured belonging, we have the same feelings: violation, anger and disbelief. In verse fourteen, he considers what happens when someone spreads false and ugly rumors about us, and we watch, helplessly, as our reputation is sullied and shredded, a possibility that, with modern technologies, can now befall anyone at any time.

Tokmé Zongpo makes a point of not seeking revenge or retribution. He takes a different approach. A person violates us because he or she is in pain. Tokmé Zongpo's advice is to connect with that person's pain and respond from there. Someone steals from you because he is in need. Imagine giving him even more. Someone slanders you because she is hurt, jealous or offended. Imagine praising her. Initially, this approach is counterintuitive. It makes little sense to the rational mind. When you actually do it, however, you come to appreciate that everyone is in pain at some level, and blindly increasing the pain in the world does not help anyone—not your enemy, nor anyone else affected, nor you.

To ease the pain in the world, you have to respond differently. You cannot rely on what your emotional reactions are telling you. You have to find clarity and presence in the situation itself, free from the projections of thought and feeling. Only then will you know what, if anything, to do.

Tokmé Zongpo's aim is to be free of the tyranny of reaction and to be awake in what is arising internally and externally. The path he describes is not a path to success as it is conventionally understood. It is a path to freedom for those who are seeking a different way of experiencing life itself.

In verses nineteen to twenty-four, Tokmé Zongpo turns

attention to specific emotional reactions and the nature of experience. Ordinarily, life is a bit like a trampoline—you bounce from one reaction to another. When you suppress reactions, you push that energy into your body. Over time, the result is suffering and illness in your body. When you give expression to your reactions, you dump that energy into the world. Others experience your emotional reactions and you do not. Through the discipline of practice you stop bouncing around and are awake in the experience of your reactions, neither suppressing them nor expressing them. Then they come and go like drawings on water. It is a tough path and the first step is to stop indulging emotional reactions. Here, Tokmé Zongpo talks about the three most important —pride, anger and desire.

Then he looks at the nature of experience itself. What is experience? You know part of the answer—it consists of thoughts, feelings and sensations. When you rest deeply, these bits of life appear and disappear like mist, a mirage or a dream in a space of timeless awareness/experience. In verse twenty-two, Tokmé Zongpo begins with that understanding and goes on from there.

Whatever arises in experience is your own mind.
Mind itself is free of any conceptual limitations.
Know that and don't entertain
Subject-object fixations—this is the practice of a bodhisattva.

When you can let the mists of life appear and disappear on their own, you discover an internal quiet, an internal space, which is always there. When you develop the ability to rest and look in that quiet you see that there is absolutely nothing there. This insight is often a shock, and when you experience it, your understanding of who and what you are changes dramatically. You see that there is no "I" as such. "I" is, itself, a collection of thoughts, feelings and sensations that come and go. Are you a constantly reconfiguring collection? Are you the space, the awareness? Are you nothing at all? Are you everything? In the face of these questions you fall silent, for there are no answers.

Up to this point in your life, you have taken your thinking and your explanations of the world very seriously. Everyone else is doing the same, too. Yet these explanations themselves are just mist that forms and reforms into different shapes and structures. They are highly contingent and context-dependent. When you live in those explanations, you are not in your actual life but in a kind of confusion, and that is where the trouble begins. You see how much struggle and pain you inflict on others and yourself because, instead of opening to the experience of life itself, you are enthralled and seduced by these explanations of life. As Tokmé Zongpo says:

All forms of suffering are like dreaming that your child
　　has died.
Taking confusion as real wears you out.

The next section, verses twenty-five to thirty, covers the six perfections, a set of practices common to all the Mahayana traditions of Buddhism. Tokmé Zongpo takes these six practices as they are traditionally presented: be generous, observe ethical behavior, cultivate patience, pour your energy into practice, cultivate stable attention, and uncover wisdom. But he makes very clear how deep each of these practices go. For generosity, he says:

If those who want to be awake have to give even their bodies,
What need is there to talk about things that you simply own?

Here he refers to the story of Buddha who, in a former life, gave his body to a tigress that was too weak to suckle her own cubs. Such mythic tales are often misinterpreted in today's world where people take everything literally. They fail to appreciate that these stories communicate through emotion, not just words. When we think of Buddha lying down in front of the tigress, cutting open his arm to allow his blood to drip into her mouth, and then letting her eat him, part of us is horrified. But another part of us is deeply moved by this extraordinary gesture of generosity, and something in us opens.

We find a similar image in the verse on effort:

Listeners and solitary buddhas, working only for their
        own welfare,
Practice as if their heads were on fire.
To help all beings, pour your energy into practice.

Again, the image touches us emotionally. When we look at the efforts people put into taking care of their own needs, material or spiritual, what are we to think of our own efforts when we are ostensibly aiming to help all beings be free of suffering? The aim here is not to shame us, but to point out the depth of the conditioning that prevents us from bringing compassion and wisdom into the way we relate to the world.

Most interpretations of the six perfections take meditative stability (verse twenty-nine) as the cultivation of the resting mind. Tokmé Zongpo takes a different approach. He regards meditative stability as a combination of resting and seeing, not just resting. Emotional reactions do stop when the mind rests, but immediately come up again when there is any movement in the mind. Only with the additional quality of insight, the direct knowing in the moment that emotional reactions are simply movement in mind, are we truly free from the tyranny of reaction.

The next five verses, thirty-one to thirty-six, cover a number of general but important points. In verse thirty-one, Tokmé Zongpo states that it is not enough just to follow the forms. The aim of practice is to resolve confusion, to open so completely to our own confusion that we find clarity in the confusion itself. In verse thirty-four, he talks about the simple but important instruction to speak gently. In the long run, gentle speech is more effective than harsh. This instruction shows up in many places, from the characteristics of right speech from the eightfold path to the four ways a bodhisattva engages people. Tokmé Zongpo took this instruction to heart. It was said that he never raised his voice in anger, never rebuked anyone and treated each and every person with respect. In verse thirty-six he ends with his summary of practice: attention, attention, attention.

> In short, in everything you do,
> Question how your mind is, moment by moment.

The last of the thirty-seven practices is about the practice of dedication, a letting go of any benefit we may derive from our spiritual practice. Dedication works on three levels. It counteracts spiritual pride and greed, it is a gesture of generosity motivated by compassion and it reminds us that nothing really belongs to us. A traditional verse of dedication expresses these three themes:

> Goodness comes from this practice now done.
> Let me not hold it just in me.
> Let it spread to all that is known
> And awaken good throughout the world.

When my own challenges pushed me to a deeper appreciation of Tokmé Zongpo's approach of "letting go of hope and fear," I started to pay more attention to what he had to say. As I taught this text, I came to appreciate more why this text is held in such high regard. However, only when I translated each verse and thought about the corresponding commentary did I come to appreciate how it reaches across time and space to speak to us today. For instance, in the third verse he talks about solitude. In Tokmé Zongpo's time, you could find quiet places to live and practice. Such solitude is much more difficult to find today, not only because of the cost of land and housing, but also because technology makes communication and entertainment accessible virtually everywhere. In today's world, the practice of solitude becomes the practice of silence, being quiet and alone and disengaging from the world of always-on communication. And, yes, when you practice silence, you do find your way.

In this book you find a way of practice, a way that enables you to understand the wisdom and experience of this path, a way in which you are not sidetracked or confused by differences in culture or language and a way that you can take into your life. It is a good place to start a study and practice of the Buddhist traditions of Tibet because it is a simple and elegant summary of Mahayana Buddhism in this tradition. Over time you may find, as I did, that each verse points to hidden depths, both in terms of how to interact with the world and how to be clear in your life.

Thirty-Seven Practices of a Bodhisattva
by Tokmé Zongpo

Namo Lokeshvaraya

HOMAGE

You who see that experience has no coming or going,
Yet pour your energy solely into helping beings,
My excellent teachers and Lord All Seeing,
I ever humbly honor with my body, speech and mind.

INTENTION

Full awakening, buddha, the source of joy and well-being,
Comes as you master the noble way.
Because mastery depends on knowing how to practice,
I now explain the practice of all bodhisattvas.

I

Right now you have a good boat, fully equipped and available—
        hard to find.
To free yourself and others from the sea of samsara,
Day and night, constantly,
Study, reflect and meditate—this is the practice of a bodhisattva.

2

Attraction to those close to you catches you in its currents;
Aversion to those who oppose you burns inside;
Indifference that ignores what needs to be done is a black hole.
Leave your homeland—this is the practice of a bodhisattva.

3

Don't engage disturbances and emotional reactions gradually
    fade away;
Don't engage distractions and spiritual practice naturally grows;
Keep awareness clear and vivid and confidence in the way arises.
Rely on silence—this is the practice of a bodhisattva.

4

You will separate from long-time friends and relatives.
You will leave behind the wealth you worked to build up.
The guest, your consciousness, will move from the inn, your body.
Give up your life—this is the practice of a bodhisattva.

5

With some friends, the three poisons keep growing,
Study, reflection and meditation weaken
While loving kindness and compassion fall away.
Give up bad friends—this is the practice of a bodhisattva.

6

With some teachers, your shortcomings fade away and
Abilities grow like the waxing moon.
Hold such teachers dear to you,
Dearer than your own body—this is the practice of a bodhisattva.

7

Locked up in the prison of their own patterning
Ordinary gods cannot protect anyone.
Where, then, do you go for refuge?
Go for refuge in what is reliable, the Three Jewels—this is the
      practice of a bodhisattva.

8

The suffering in the lower realms is extremely hard to endure.
The Sage says it is the result of destructive actions.
For that reason, even if your life is at risk,
Don't engage in destructive actions—this is the practice of
      a bodhisattva.

9

The happiness of the three worlds disappears in a moment,
Like a dewdrop on a blade of grass.
The highest level of freedom is one that never changes.
Aim for this—this is the practice of a bodhisattva.

10

Every being has cared for you as your mother.
If they all suffer for time without end, how can you be happy?
To free beings without limit,
Give rise to awakening mind—this is the practice of a bodhisattva.

11

All suffering comes from wanting your own happiness.
Complete awakening arises from the intention to help others.
Therefore, exchange completely your happiness
For the suffering of others—this is the practice of a bodhisattva.

12

Even if someone, driven by desperate want,
Steals or makes someone else steal everything you own,
Dedicate to him your body, your wealth and
All the good you have ever done or will do—this is the practice of
a bodhisattva.

13

Even if you have done nothing wrong at all
And someone still tries to take your head off,
Spurred by compassion
Take all his or her venom into you—this is the practice of
a bodhisattva.

14

Even if someone broadcasts to the whole universe
Slanderous and ugly rumors about you,
Again and again, with an open and caring heart,
Praise his or her abilities—this is the practice of a bodhisattva.

15

Even if someone humiliates you and denounces you
In front of a crowd of people,
Think of this person as your teacher
And humbly honor him—this is the practice of a bodhisattva.

16

Even if a person you have cared for as your own child
Treats you as her worst enemy,
Lavish her with loving attention
Like a mother caring for her ill child—this is the practice of
a bodhisattva.

17

Even if your peers or those below you
Put you down to make themselves look better,
Treat them respectfully as if they were your teacher:
Put them above you—this is the practice of a bodhisattva.

18

When you are down and out, held in contempt,
Desperately ill and emotionally crazed,
Don't lose heart. Take into you
The suffering and negativity of all beings—this is the practice of
    a bodhisattva.

19

Even when you are famous, honored by all
And as rich as the god of wealth himself,
Know that success in the world is ephemeral
And don't let it go to your head—this is the practice of
    a bodhisattva.

20

If you don't subdue the enemy inside—your own anger—
The more enemies you subdue outside, the more that come.
Muster the forces of loving kindness and compassion,
And subdue your own mind—this is the practice of a bodhisattva.

21

Sensual pleasures are like salty water:
The deeper you drink, the thirstier you become.
Any object you attach to,
Right away, let it go—this is the practice of a bodhisattva.

22

Whatever arises in experience is your own mind.
Mind itself is free of any conceptual limitations.
Know that and don't entertain
Subject-object fixations—this is the practice of a bodhisattva.

23

When you come across something you enjoy,
Though beautiful to experience, like a summer rainbow,
Don't take it as real.
Let go of attachment—this is the practice of a bodhisattva.

24

All forms of suffering are like dreaming that your child has died.
Taking confusion as real wears you out.
When you run into misfortune,
Look at it as confusion—this is the practice of a bodhisattva.

25

If those who want to be awake have to give even their bodies,
What need is there to talk about things that you simply own?
Be generous without looking
For any return or result—this is the practice of a bodhisattva.

26

If you cannot look after yourself because you have no ethical
        discipline,
Then your intention to take care of others is simply a joke.
Observe ethical behavior without concern
For a conventional life—this is the practice of a bodhisattva.

27

For bodhisattvas who want to be rich in virtue
A person who hurts you is a precious treasure.
Cultivate patience for everyone,
Without irritation or resentment—this is the practice of
      a bodhisattva.

28

Listeners and solitary buddhas, working only for their
      own welfare,
Practice as if their heads were on fire.
To help all beings, pour your energy into practice:
It is the source of all abilities—this is the practice of a bodhisattva.

29

Understanding that emotional reactions are dismantled
By insight supported by stillness,
Cultivate meditative stability that passes right by
The four formless states—this is the practice of a bodhisattva.

30

Without wisdom, the five perfections
Are not enough to attain full awakening.
Cultivate wisdom and skill
Free from the three domains—this is the practice of a bodhisattva.

31

If you don't go into your own confusion,
You may be just a materialist in practitioner's clothing.
Constantly go into your own confusion
And put an end to it—this is the practice of a bodhisattva.

32

You undermine yourself when you react emotionally and
Grumble about the imperfections of other bodhisattvas.
Of the imperfections of those who have entered the Great Way,
Don't say anything—this is the practice of a bodhisattva.

33

When you squabble with others about status and rewards,
You undermine learning, reflection and meditation.
Let go of any investment in your family circle
Or the circle of those who support you—this is the practice of
    a bodhisattva.

34

Abusive language upsets others
And undermines the ethics of a bodhisattva.
Don't upset people or
Speak abusively—this is the practice of a bodhisattva.

35

When emotional reactions build up momentum, it is hard to
    make remedies work.
A present and aware person uses remedies as weapons
To crush craving and other emotional reactions
As soon as they arise—this is the practice of a bodhisattva.

36

In short, in everything you do,
Question how your mind is, moment by moment.
By being constantly present and aware
You bring about what helps others—this is the practice of
    a bodhisattva.

37

To dispel the suffering of beings without limit,
With wisdom freed from the three domains
Direct all the goodness generated by these efforts
To awakening—this is the practice of a bodhisattva.

SOURCE

Following the teachings of the holy ones
On what is written in the sutras, tantras and commentaries,
I set out these thirty-seven practices of a bodhisattva
For those who intend to train in this path.

AUTHORITY

Because I have limited intelligence and little education,
These verses are not the kind of poetry that pleases the learned.
But because I relied on the teachings of the sutras and the revered,
I am confident that *The Practices of a Bodhisattva* is sound.

SHORTCOMINGS

However, because it is hard for a person like me with limited
    intelligence
To fathom the profundity of the great waves of the activity
    of bodhisattvas,
I ask the revered to tolerate any mistakes I have made,
Contradictions, non sequiturs, and such.

DEDICATION

Through the goodness of this work may all beings,
In awakening to both what seems and is true,
Not rest in any limiting position—existence or peace:
May they become equal to Great Compassion.

Tokmé the monk, a teacher of scripture and logic, composed this text in a cave near the town of Ngülchu Rinchen for his own and others' benefit.

Namo Lokeshvaraya

WHAT INSPIRES YOU TO PRACTICE?

In keeping with Tibetan tradition, Tokmé Zongpo begins with a Sanskrit homage. In this case, the homage is to Lokeshvara, Lord of the World, a mythic figure, the embodiment of awakened compassion in medieval Indian Buddhism.

Imagine that you are Lokeshvara. Inside you are as quiet as a pond that lies in the center of a deep forest, a pond that, protected by the trees around it, has been undisturbed by even the slightest breeze for a thousand years. Feel that stillness within you.

Because of that stillness, you hear everything. You hear the cry of a baby when it first comes into the world. You hear a young woman's gasp of disbelief and despair when her boyfriend breaks things off. You hear the sobs of pain of a woman stricken by breast cancer. You hear the sigh of a man when he first realizes that his body is losing its vitality. And you hear the rasping breath of those whose time in the world has come to an end. You hear the sufferings and struggles of those brought low by misfortune, bad luck or their own folly. You hear the cries of those who are oppressed, exploited or abused. You hear the pain in the voices of those who oppress, exploit or abuse others. You hear the suffering of the world.

What do you do?

In the stillness, your heart breaks and out pours a river of compassion. You reach out and touch the pain of each and every person. Whatever the connection, you find a way to ease their pain. In that easing, each person knows a moment of open stillness, a quiet they have never experienced before, and that moment changes everything.

This is why he is called Lord of the World.

You who see that experience has no coming or going,
Yet pour your energy solely into helping beings,
My excellent teachers and Lord All Seeing,
I ever humbly honor with my body, speech and mind.

IMAGINE THAT YOU ARE LOOKING AT A TREE. IT IS A windy day. You feel the gusts against your cheeks. You hear the rustle of the leaves. Even the biggest branches sway in the wind. You see the branches sway, you hear the wind in the leaves, but there is no movement—not inside, not outside, not anywhere.

Now imagine that you could experience your thoughts and feelings the same way. They come and they go, but for you there is no movement, none at all. It doesn't matter what arises—love, anger, need, pride, grief, joy—you experience it, you experience it all, yet there is no disturbance in you, no movement whatsoever— no coming or going. It is possible to experience life this way. When you do, you experience a freedom that you cannot put into words.

If you had this experience, what difference would it make for you? How would it change the way you see others, particularly when you see them locked in beliefs, flooded by emotions or afire in their obsessions? Do you not want to reach out and ease the pain, even when you know there is little, if any, actual help you can give?

This is the essence of compassion. It arises in that profound and indescribable stillness and it reaches out to ease the pain of the world. It is what Lokeshvara represents, or, as he is also known,

Avalokiteshvara, the lord who sees everything. It is what motivates your teachers. It leads them to forego more conventional lives and give their time and energy to helping others find and follow a path to freedom.

Spiritual practice often begins with awe, the feeling of being intimately connected to something that is infinitely greater than you. When you read these pages, take a moment to touch the compassion that Lokeshvara embodies. Then touch the awe you feel when you do. You may be moved to bow your head, or to offer something in thought, word or deed. Whatever practice you do, begin with awe—awe that makes your jaw drop, brings tears to your eyes, silences all thinking and stills your heart—awe at this extraordinary compassion, the compassion your teachers live and the potential for compassion that lies in you.

Full awakening, buddha, the source of joy and well-being,
Comes as you master the noble way.
Because mastery depends on knowing how to practice,
I now explain the practice of all bodhisattvas.

SOME PEOPLE LEARN BY STUDYING. OTHERS LEARN
by listening. Some people learn by systematic doing. Others learn
by playing.

Have you given any thought to how you learn, or do you usually
just accept the teaching formats presented to you?

For instance, listening to talks does not work for me, which is
a bit ironic, because I have given more than a few talks. Even so,
I move into question-and-answer mode whenever possible. That
is what works for me, both as a student and as a teacher. I learn
when I can ask questions and I teach best when I am responding
to questions.

But that is not the case for everyone.

Some people learn better by listening. They take in what the
speaker or teacher says. They just absorb it. I find that amazing,
but they seem to do very well that way.

Others like to mess around with stuff—play with it. It may not
be systematic, but it is how most hackers and computer geeks and
tech wizards started, not to mention any number of scientists and
quite a few musicians, artists and writers.

A sword master taught a student by giving him a long wooden
stick and telling him to carry it at all times, even when he was
doing chores or sleeping or relieving himself. The master then
attacked the student unexpectedly time and again. The student had

to avoid the blows and defend himself as best he could. Although he never learned any theory, postures, strikes or strategies, the student became a superb swordsman.

In traditional societies, a lot of learning took place by just watching. When you studied with a master sushi chef, you cleaned knives while the chef worked. But you watched. You paid attention. After three to five years, you were finally allowed to pick up a knife. You could cut properly almost right away because your body had taken in how to hold and move the knife. Renaissance master artists used the same method with brushes instead of knives. This method is rarely used these days. People say they do not have the time, but the learning that takes place is deep and lasting.

Others do best with a course of study, learning one topic, assimilating it, then learning the next, a sequential progression that results in mastery of a curriculum. This, of course, is how modern education works. This kind of system develops when you have a well-defined process aimed at a specific result.

In Tibet, traditional monastic training used exactly this approach. The education and training system for monks was laid out, beginning with learning the phonetic alphabet, then how to spell words, then how to say them, then learning what they meant, then engaging in debate to learn how to think, etc. This is probably how Tokmé Zongpo was taught, but his natural abilities put him ahead of the game.

The same methodical approach was applied to spiritual training. The *lam-rim* genre in Tibetan Buddhism, on which *Thirty-Seven Practices* is based, presents the canonical material of Tibetan Buddhism in a well-defined sequence. Beginning with motivation, you are taught step by step how to relate to a teacher, to solitude, to morality and to refuge. Then come the four immeasurables and awakening mind; then you are led through the six perfections and conclude with the bodhisattva stages, buddhahood and buddha activity.

It is thorough. It is comprehensive. It is solid. But is it how you learn and is it how you learn to practice?

Here is a suggestion: find a teacher, someone with whom you can really learn, whose teaching style works with your learning style.

Right now you have a good boat, fully equipped and
    available—hard to find.
To free yourself and others from the sea of samsara,
Day and night, constantly,
Study, reflect and meditate—this is the practice of
    a bodhisattva.

YOU ARE STANDING ON A WOODEN DOCK. IT IS OLD
and falling apart. In front of you, the open expanse of the ocean
extends to the horizon. Below your feet is a boat, well stocked and
fully equipped. You know it is, because you took care in preparing it.

It is the only boat at the dock. The other moorings are empty,
forgotten.

You are not exactly sure how you came to be here, but you do
know you cannot turn your back on the ocean. Yet you hesitate to
step into the boat.

What stops you?

From the town behind you, you hear a constant hum of activity: cars, buses, people crying their wares in the market, the faint
wail of an ambulance, a police car or a fire truck racing to the next
emergency. You know that your friends, your colleagues and your
relatives are all busy—providing for their families, moving ahead
in their lives, making their mark in the world.

You are here looking at the ocean, the boat gently bobbing at
your feet as waves lap against the dock.

The world behind you seems simultaneously full and empty.
There are many enjoyments and rewards. You have tasted them.
But you cannot escape a sense of futility and a gnawing insistence

that wonders, "Is this all there is?" Your friends sometimes touch the same feeling, but they turn away from it quickly—a gap in the web of life that is never explored.

You cannot turn away. You wonder how they can. And you wonder what, if anything, you can do for them so that they do not turn away. You wonder because you are pretty sure that you are missing something, and that is why you prepared the boat. And you think they may be missing something, too. But you do not know what.

What will it take for you to step into the boat?

Attraction to those close to you catches you in its currents;
Aversion to those who oppose you burns inside;
Indifference that ignores what needs to be done is a
     black hole.
Leave your homeland—this is the practice of a bodhisattva.

DO YOU REALLY HAVE TO MOVE TO ANOTHER COUNTRY in order to practice?

Perhaps you have already gone to a retreat or a meditation program on the other side of the world, but you probably bought a round-trip ticket.

You arrive full of enthusiasm, unpack your carry-on, set up your meditation cushion and roll out your yoga mat. After a couple of days you discover a few unwanted items came with you, items that you do not remember packing.

During breaks, you flirt with the person who sits in front of you. You find the person who sits on the cushion beside you unbearable. Why did he have to sit right there? Why does he have to wear such bright colors? Others you just ignore because you do not need them, and you expect they feel the same way about you. The food, your accommodations and even the scenery you like, or dislike, or it fails to move you one way or the other.

Attraction, aversion and indifference—the three poisons. You traveled thousands of miles to be free from them, and here they are now as if you had never left home.

These basic patterns poison your life. You cannot just enjoy something—you have to have it. You cannot just meet a challenge—you have to oppose it. You cannot just relax—you have to check out.

These poisons pull you out of present experience and into the past, an eternal limbo in which you forever seek the love you always wanted and fight with the ghosts of those who stood in your way. When nothing touches you, your indifference creates a distance between you and the world around you. It is not so easy to leave your homeland.

There are other possibilities.

One. Bring attention to the feeling tones that accompany every sensory experience—pleasant, unpleasant and neutral. Feel how the three reactions—attraction, aversion and indifference—move in you. They are fast. They are insistent. They are insidious. As you keep doing this, your relationship with these three poisons gradually changes.

Two. When you feel attraction starting to run, breathe in and take in the same attraction, first from everyone you know, then from everyone in the world. What do you have to lose? The attraction is already running in you. You are already messed up. You might as well take in the poison from others and set them free. Ditto for aversion. Ditto for indifference.

Three. When you see someone or something you like, open to the whole experience, the person or object and the attraction in you. With attraction, you are aware of every detail in the person or the object. Rest right there. With aversion, your mind becomes very clear. Rest there. With indifference, you are aware of everything. Rest there.

When you are able to experience these poisons and not act on them, you have left your homeland.

Safe travels? Not likely.

Don't engage disturbances and emotional reactions
    gradually fade away;
Don't engage distractions and spiritual practice
    naturally grows;
Keep awareness clear and vivid and confidence in the
    way arises.
Rely on silence—this is the practice of a bodhisattva.

HOW MANY WORLDS DO YOU GO TO EVERY DAY? EVERY disturbance, every emotional reaction, projects a different world. Like a flea on a hot stove, you jump from one world to another. Never mind jet lag, you are a different person in each world. Alice had an easier time in Wonderland.

How do you find your path?
In silence.

How do you practice silence?
You listen.

Arrange your life to reduce choice and unnecessary decisions. Refrain from taking on too many projects at one time. When you are involved in a lot of different activities, the demands from one create problems for another. In other words, create the conditions so that you do not have to be reacting to a steady stream of disturbances.

When you practice, rest in the experience of thoughts, sensations and feelings, using the breath or awareness itself as a place to rest. Whenever you are carried away, return and rest. During practice sessions regard thoughts, sensations and feelings as leaves swirling in the wind as you walk under the clear blue sky of an autumn day. When you do not engage them, you become aware of a silence—a silence that is always there, even in your darkest moments, a silence that includes everything and cannot be fathomed, a silence that allows you to listen to your heart, your body and your mind in a way you did not know was possible.

In that silence awareness is clear and vivid. You just know, and a quiet confidence is born.

How do you find your way? In silence.

You will separate from long-time friends and relatives.
You will leave behind the wealth you worked to build up.
The guest, your consciousness, will move from the inn,
    your body.
Give up your life—this is the practice of a bodhisattva.

CONSIDER FOR A MOMENT THAT YOU COULD DIE AT
any moment—in the next minute, today, tomorrow—or months
or years down the line. Does your body tense or relax, or does
something else happen? What feelings arise—fear or relief, anger
or longing, guilt, hope, resignation or equanimity?

Even a little reflection along these lines brings up strong reactions. Your body does everything it can to stay alive. When your life
is threatened, it reacts—strongly. Fear and panic seize you. Fight,
flee or freeze—the basic survival tactics take over. Even when you
face other kinds of death—the end of a relationship or the loss of
your job—the same mechanisms run. You are conditioned to live,
biologically and psychologically.

You know you are going to die, but you do not believe it. You
ignore the fact that death is inevitable. You focus your time and
energy on the conventional concerns—happiness, gain, respect
and reputation—for these are what give meaning to most people's lives.

However, if you are reading this book, you are looking for
something beyond the conventional. As Robinson Jeffers writes:

...only
tormented persons want truth.

Man is like other animals, wants food and success and women,
not truth. Only if the mind
Tortured by some interior tension has despaired of happiness:
then it hates
its life-cage and seeks further…

If you want a bit of truth, then start with The Four Ends:

The end of accumulation is dispersion.
The end of building is ruin.
The end of meeting is parting.
The end of birth is death.

Nothing is permanent. Everything is constantly changing.
Everything is in the process of becoming something that it is cur-
rently not—including you. Some changes take place quickly, at the
speed of light. Others take place over such vast expanses of time
that they are all but imperceptible. Everything in the world, everything you experience, grows and evolves, often in predictable ways,
but unavoidable all the same. Yet chance occurrences, the unpredictable, can enrich, diminish, destroy or transform your life in
an instant.

Most people do not acknowledge just how much of their lives
is pure luck, good or bad. They take credit when they happen to be
at the right place at the right time, meet the right person or say the
right words. They tend to look for someone or something to blame
when they are in the wrong place at the wrong time, or meet the
wrong person or say the wrong words.

Another bit of truth: the course of your life can change in a
heartbeat, whether or not you do everything right or everything
wrong.

Given that, how do you live this experience we call life?

Give up your life. Give it all up. Do not base your life on what
can be taken away from you—wealth, possessions, health, family,

friends, fame, respect, even your own life. If you have the good fortune to have family, friends, wealth or respect, savor them, knowing that they all must come to an end, sooner or later. But do not base your life on holding on to them.

Instead, do what life calls for in each moment, and do so without any gaining idea, any thought that you will ever see or enjoy the results of your actions. Do it because your life calls for it—nothing more.

Ironically, it is hard to imagine a more fulfilling way to live.

What happens to the guest? No one knows. It is a mystery.

With some friends, the three poisons keep growing,
Study, reflection and meditation weaken
While loving kindness and compassion fall away.
Give up bad friends—this is the practice of a bodhisattva.

LIKE ATTRACTS LIKE. ANGER REINFORCES ANGER.
Greed begets greed. Indifference breeds indifference.

Your circle of friends and associates reflects your values, your
behaviors and how you experience life.

You also know the power of peer pressure, the power of domi-
nation and the power of inclusion and exclusion. You experienced
it in school, you experience it at work and you encounter it in every
social context.

It is the same internally, too. Which stories about you or your
life do you repeat to yourself over and over again? Which behaviors
do you nourish, indulge or ignore?

You want to change how you experience life, but you may not
want anything else to change. Is that possible? Sooner or later, you
have to face this squarely.

Take a look around you. Look at your friends and associates.
Ask yourself, "Is this how I want to behave? Is this how I want to
live? Is this how I want to be?"

Look inside, too, and ask, "Is this how I want to be thinking
and feeling?"

If the answer is no, then you begin.

Start with what is inside you. When you find yourself repeating

45

the same behavior over and over again, give it a name. Learn to recognize that behavior and call it by its name. When you name something, it loses power. Just ask Rumpelstiltskin.

Little by little you change. You do not enjoy bantering the way you used to. You find it jarring, unkind and mindless. The old haunts, the old interests, the usual topics of conversation engage you less and less. You feel you are a performer, putting on a bit of an act to be one of the gang. You are not sure how much longer you can keep it up.

At some point, you stop trying. You let it all drop.

There is loss, definitely, and with loss there is grief, the pain of separating from patterns and people. Yet you feel lighter and clearer, as if you had set down a coat or a mask that you had been wearing for no apparent reason.

A caution. As these changes unfold, you may see your new direction as better, as superior, to your old ways. That is only natural, but it is easy to fall into another old habit—criticizing and disparaging the friends and the ways of life you are leaving behind.

If you find yourself becoming critical and judgmental, let it go. You are falling back into old patterns—exactly what you wanted to leave behind.

VERSE 6

With some teachers, your shortcomings fade away and
Abilities grow like the waxing moon.
Hold such teachers dear to you,
Dearer than your own body—this is the practice of
a bodhisattva.

FOR MANY, ONE OF THE BIGGEST CHALLENGES IN
spiritual practice is to find a teacher or guide.

Whatever discipline or training you seek, the teacher embodies
in some way what you want to know or how you want to be. Why
else would you study with this person?

Good teachers are hard to find. Fame is not a good criterion.
In most cases, those who become famous have to cooperate with
the forces that propel them to fame, and they are usually bent in
the process. Many people seek out those who are famous, as a
kind of credential, but there is another problem. As Yogi Berra
said of a famous restaurant, "Nobody goes there anymore. It's too
crowded."

Look at a teacher's students. You will learn much about a
teacher from them.

Look for a person who speaks to you, someone to whom you
will listen even when you are completely crazy.

When you find a teacher who embodies what you seek, cultivate that relationship and take care of it. Like any relationship, it
takes work.

The teacher shows you possibilities, trains you in the skills and
abilities you need and points out your internal material when it
gets in the way. Your responsibility is to make sure you understand

what you are learning and make use of what the teacher gives you without corrupting or editing it.

When you do study with someone, pay attention not only to what you *intend* to learn, but to what you *are* learning. Like every relationship, the one between teacher and student is a mystery. The teacher may teach you skills and train you in abilities that neither you nor he ever intended. You cannot predict what actually happens.

If he listens carefully to you, you learn how to listen, whether or not you wanted to learn how to listen. If she gives traditional answers to your questions, you learn how to give traditional answers, whether that was her intention or not. If she challenges you and pushes you beyond what you think you can do, you learn to challenge others and push them beyond what they think they can do. If he is short and impatient, you learn how to be short and impatient.

If communication seems to break down, do not assume that there is a problem. The teacher may be showing you possibilities that you never imagined.

In the presence of a capable spiritual teacher, your emotional reactivity subsides and you are able to be with parts of yourself that you could never face before. You experience a peace, a clarity, an energy—a freedom that you did not know was possible. Do not make the mistake of believing that such shifts are solely dependent on the teacher. They come about because you are present in a higher level of energy and attention, capabilities that your teacher has developed and you are there to develop.

If you see such shifts as dependent on your teacher, you inevitably end up worshipping him or her, and that does neither of you any good.

Cherish the relationship, but do not worship your teacher. He or she has foibles, too. When you ignore them, you are living in a world of your own projections. You are not relating or connecting with the person who is in front of you.

Do not speak badly of your teacher, either, even if you come to part ways. There is no surer way to undermine your own practice or to close a door to your own awakening.

Do not try to be a friend to your teacher, and do not regard him or her as a friend. Friendship may evolve. It often does. But that is not the point of the relationship. The point is to learn what you need to, in terms of possibilities, skills and what gets in your way.

It is often more difficult to find a good teacher than it is to find a suitable partner. When you find one, take care of the relationship. Listen to the instructions, engage with your teacher to make sure you understand them, take them to heart and put them into practice.

Locked up in the prison of their own patterning
Ordinary gods cannot protect anyone.
Where, then, do you go for refuge?
Go for refuge in what is reliable, the Three Jewels—this is
    the practice of a bodhisattva.

TO WHAT DO YOU TRUST YOUR LIFE? TO PUT IT ANOTHER way, who are your gods?

For many the answer is money. Most people feel that if they have enough money, they will be safe and happy, because they believe that with money they can have security, comfort, respect, power or fame. They place their trust in money. Money is their god, their refuge.

What about happiness? A fleeting and capricious goddess, she visits you briefly whenever something changes for the better, then slips away a few days later. Sometimes you find happiness when you least expect her, when you are challenged in every possible way and are fully and completely engaged in life. Ironically, when everything is going smoothly, you often find that ennui has taken her place.

Other popular gods are power, physical beauty, sex appeal, longevity, moral purity, knowledge, integrity and courage. You may look to family and community, health and fitness or bliss and other transcendent experiences for your security or identity.

Gods are projections of your hopes and desires, but your hopes and desires are themselves projections of emotional patterns, projections of the past, projections of what you feel is missing in you, of what you feel will make you complete or accord you a place in the world. Can a pattern free you?

A pattern is a ghost from the past. It cannot help you. The world that generated it no longer exists. Whenever it runs, it draws you into the illusion of that world. If you try to satisfy it, you have accepted that world, and you are in its power, with all its demands, dysfunctions and contradictions. This is the opposite of the freedom you seek.

You need a direction. Traditionally, that is the Buddha, an example of how to live free from struggle. You need a way, a path. You find your path through the Dharma, the understanding and experience of those who have made similar journeys. You need guides, the Sangha, those who share your intention, serve as examples and can point out what works and where the pitfalls are.

In the end, however, all you have is awareness, the quality of knowing that is present in every moment of experience—indefinable, indescribable, non-conceptual knowing. It seems to be nothing at all, yet it is there—clear and present—and experience just arises, without restriction. Can you trust that knowing? Can you trust that clarity? Can you trust your own experience?

To look at it from another perspective, refuge is about how you relate to the experience of life itself. When you stop looking outside or inside for something to free you from your struggles, you take refuge in direct awareness. That is buddha. When awareness and experience are not different, you stop struggling with what arises and you are taking refuge in clarity. That is dharma. And when you experience life without grasping, opposing or ignoring what arises, you take refuge in unrestricted experience. That is sangha.

The suffering in the lower realms is extremely hard to endure.
The Sage says it is the result of destructive actions.
For that reason, even if your life is at risk,
Don't engage in destructive actions—this is the practice of
a bodhisattva.

THE LOWER REALMS ARE THE WORLDS PROJECTED BY
anger, greed and survival—the worlds of your most basic instincts,
the worlds where your only options are to fight or flee, to eat or be
eaten, to kill or die.

When was the last time you were seized by anger?
A colleague at work makes an offhand comment, a little disrespectful in your opinion. Something in you suddenly switches, and
you are seething—your body hot and flushed, your stomach knotted and churning. A string of four-letter words pours out of your
mouth. You have no idea what you are saying. You are standing
now, looking down on him, breathing heavily, teeth clenched. He
looks startled, alarmed, and quickly leaves the room.
What happened?

Go back to it now. As best you can, recall the feeling of anger.
What happens in your body? Is there a red-hot iron rod burning
you from the inside out? Are red-hot rocks crashing together in
your guts? Are you swirling in a vat of molten copper? Welcome to
the realms of the hot hells!
What about hatred? Most people do not acknowledge it. It is
too cold, too unfeeling. When you are utterly hard and inflexible,

cold and rigid, you are in the grip of hatred. If you move even a millimeter, you crack and break. If you put your hand on your heart, you can feel how hard and cold it is. This is a world of hard, cold, rigid ice. As Robert Frost wrote:

Some say the world will end in fire,
Some say in ice....

The world of greed is not much better. What happens when you think about money? Does your body tense up? Do your hands start to clench? When you think of something you feel you need, can you feel the desperation, the fear, the grasping. Listen to the stories. "If I don't get this, then..."

When you fall into any of these realms, you do not know what you are doing, let alone what you are feeling or experiencing. Stories, justifications and rationalizations take you over. You do not notice even vivid physical and emotional sensations. You do not feel the pain you are in, yet, through your actions, through your words, you visit that pain on others.

Every thought, word and deed sets in motion a process that shapes the way you experience life. Whatever you put into the world comes back to you, one way or another. When you lose your temper or, out of greed and desperation, you take more than your share, you cause pain for others and set in motion the ruination of your own life. Destructive actions indeed!

It is not enough to say you will be good or you will not behave badly. Notice how old you feel when you say, "I'll be good." This is a child's approach to life. It is based on old patterns of seeking parental attention and affection and avoiding punishment.

Forget about being good or bad. Bring attention to your life. Experience what is actually happening in you. Know what you are doing and how it affects others.

Some destructive behaviors are so deeply conditioned that you cannot imagine doing something different. Even if you do, it feels like death. It is death, a dying to the world of the emotional reaction.

You have a choice: let your emotional reactions destroy your life and the lives of others or die to the realms generated by these reactions. Which do you choose?

The happiness of the three worlds disappears in a moment,
Like a dewdrop on a blade of grass.
The highest level of freedom is one that never changes.
Aim for this—this is the practice of a bodhisattva.

THE PURSUIT OF HAPPINESS FOR ITS OWN SAKE IS
a fool's errand. As a goal it is frivolous and unrealistic—frivolous
because happiness is a transient state dependent on many conditions, and unrealistic because life is unpredictable and pain may
arise at anytime.

The happiness you feel when you get something you have
always wanted typically lasts no longer than three days. Bliss
states in meditation are similar, whether they arise as physical or
emotional bliss or the bliss of infinite space, infinite consciousness or infinite nothingness. These states soon dissipate once you
re-engage the messiness of life. A dewdrop on a blade of grass,
indeed!

The quest for happiness is a continuation of the traditional
view of spiritual practice—a way to transcend the vicissitudes of
the human condition. Valhalla, paradise, heaven, nirvana all hold
out a promise of eternity, bliss, purity or union with an ultimate
reality. These four spiritual longings are all escapist reactions to
the challenges everyone encounters in life.

Take a moment and think about what you are seeking in your
practice. Is it a kind of transcendence, if not in God, then in a god-
surrogate such as timeless awareness, pure bliss or infinite light?

Are you looking for an awareness so deep and powerful that your frustration and difficulties with life vanish in the presence of your understanding and wisdom? Are you not looking for a ticket out of the messiness of life?

If you think of freedom as a state, you are in effect looking for a kind of heaven. Instead, think of freedom as a way of experiencing life itself—a continuous flow in which you meet what arises in your experience, open to it, do what needs to be done to the best of your ability and then receive the result. And you do this over and over again. A freedom that never changes then becomes the constant exercise of everything you know and understand. It is the way you engage life. It is not something that sets you apart from life. How else is it possible for people who practice in prison or other highly restricted environments to say that they find freedom even within their confinement?

Life is tough, but when you see and accept what is actually happening, even if it is very difficult or painful, mind and body relax. There is an exquisite quality that comes from just experiencing what arises, completely, with no separation between awareness and experience.

Some call it joy, but it is not a giddy or excited joy. It is deep and quiet, a joy that in some sense is always there, waiting for you, but usually touched only when some challenge, pain or tragedy leaves you with no other option but to open and accept what is happening in your life.

Others call it truth, but this is a loaded and misleading word, carrying with it the notion of something that exists apart from experience itself. Truth as a concept sets up an opposition with what is held to be not true, and such duality necessarily leads to hierarchical authority, institutional thinking and violence.

In this freedom you are free from the projections of thought and feeling, and you are awake and present in your life. Reactions may still arise, but they come and go on their own, like snowflakes alighting on a hot stone, like mist in the morning sun or like a thief in an empty house.

What is freedom? It is nothing more, and nothing less, than life lived awake.

Every being has cared for you as your mother.
If they all suffer for time without end, how can you be happy?
To free beings without limit,
Give rise to awakening mind—this is the practice of
      a bodhisattva.

WHAT IS AWAKENING MIND?

Take a moment and consider all the beings in the world—people in every walk of life, animals, even insects—billions upon billions. Each and every being is just like you—struggling with life in different ways, struggling to survive, struggling with change or struggling to make sense of it all.

Imagine you have the ability to free all these beings from their struggles and from the pain those struggles cause them. Now imagine you do free them, one by one, over the course of countless eons, no matter how long it takes.

While you embrace the possibility of freeing countless beings over countless eons, recall that there are no beings. All those beings and all your efforts are just your experience of life, nothing more and nothing less.

Everything drops away. Rest right there—in that open clarity. Nothing at all, but what a nothing!

This is awakening mind.

From this empty clarity, open to the world, to the whole universe. You see joy and pain, beauty and ugliness, love and hate, confusion and wisdom, and everything in between—the whole panorama of the human condition.

What do you feel? A mixture—peace and freedom on the one

hand, sadness and compassion on the other. In your heart is a longing, a yearning, to help all beings find a way to live in which they are not struggling with their lives, not driven by emotional reactions, not confused and bewildered about who and what they are and why they are here.

This also is awakening mind.

In the Tibetan tradition, you cultivate that intention by considering every being to be your mother—infinite mothers caring for you over the course of infinite lifetimes, a poetic expression of the vast and intricate web of relationships that make up our lives.

Look at the places where you struggle in your life. In each you see some form of alienation, a painful memory, an unpleasant association, an old fear. Every one of those parts of you is based in a relationship. Whenever you encounter a situation that resonates with that relationship, it brings that part into play, and you struggle. You cannot be free until all those parts of you are free, too. All those relationships, all those beings, all those reactions!

In the Zen tradition, the longing and the intention to free and be free take expression in The Four Great Vows:

Beings are numberless: may I free them all.
Reactions are endless: may I release them all.
Doors to experience are infinite: may I enter them all.
Ways of awakening are limitless: may I know them all.

You interact with others who are lost in confusion—countless beings. Every interaction triggers a reaction in you—endless reactions. Every time a reaction releases, that is, you are able to be aware in the experience of the reaction until it lets go, a door opens, a door to something you could not experience before—infinitely many doors. And every door leads you to awaken to another dimension of life—limitless awakenings.

All suffering comes from wanting your own happiness.
Complete awakening arises from the intention to help others.
Therefore, exchange completely your happiness
For the suffering of others—this is the practice of
    a bodhisattva.

FORGET ABOUT BEING HAPPY. PUT IT RIGHT OUT OF
your mind.

When you say to yourself, "I want to be happy," you are telling
yourself that you are not happy and you start looking for something that will make you feel happy. You go to a movie, go shop-
ping, hang out with friends, buy a new jacket, computer, or jewelry, read a good book or explore a new hobby, all in the effort to
feel happy. The harder you try to be happy, the more you reinforce
that belief that you are not happy. You can try to ignore it, but the
belief is still there.

Even in close relationships, spending time with a friend, helping others or doing other good works, if your attention is on what
you are feeling, on what you are getting out of it, then you see these
relationships as transactions. Because your focus is on how you are
feeling, consciously or unconsciously, you are putting yourself first
and others second.

This approach disconnects you from life, from the totality of
your world. Inevitably, you end up feeling short-changed in your
relationships with your family, with your friends and in your work.
Those imbalances ripple out and affect everyone around you and
beyond. The transactional mindset of self-interest is the problem
of the modern world.

If you let go of the pursuit of happiness, what would you do? To put it a bit more dramatically, suppose you were told that, no matter what you did, you would never be happy. Never. What would you do with your life?

You might pay more attention to others. You might accept them just as they are, rather than looking for ways to get them to conform to your idea of how they should be. You might start relating to life itself, rather than looking to what you get out of it. You might be more willing to engage with what life brings you, with all its ups and downs, rather than always wanting it to be other than it is.

This is where the practice of taking and sending comes in. Take in what you do not want and give away what you do want. Take in what is unpleasant and give away what is pleasant. Take in pain and give away joy.

It sounds a bit insane—emotional suicide, as one person put it. But it counteracts that deeply ingrained tendency to focus on you first, and everyone else second. It uses the transactional attitude to destroy itself because you give away everything that makes you feel happy and you take in everything that makes others unhappy.

In the traditional teachings you coordinate taking and sending with the breath, taking in the pain and suffering of the world as you breathe in, and sending your own joy and happiness to the world when you breathe out. Do this with every aspect of your life —the good and the bad, the ugly and the beautiful. Extend it to everything you experience, internally and externally.

When you see other people struggling, whatever the reason, imagine taking in their struggles and sending them your own experience of peace, happiness and joy. It does not matter who they are—the rich, the poor, the ill or the criminal. If they are struggling, take in their struggles and send them the joy, happiness or well-being you do experience, have experienced or hope to experience. If they are in pain, take in their pain. Send them your relief and ease. If they are causing pain, take in the emotional turmoil or the willful ignoring that leads them to inflict pain on others. Send them the love, compassion and understanding that you have received or would like to receive.

Do not edit your experience of life. Whatever you encounter—a homeless person shivering on an icy concrete doorsill, a friend whose partner has just left him for someone else, a relative who struggles with chronic pain, news of famine, war, or the devastating effects of greed, corruption or rigid beliefs—whatever the pain, take it in.

Do not be miserly. Give to others anything and everything that brings you joy. Are you successful in your work? Give away your success. Do you have money in the bank? Send the joy of financial well-being to others. Do you enjoy your intelligence, your ability to think clearly and solve problems? Give them away. Are you talented, musically, physically or artistically? Give away your talent. Do you enjoy friends and companions? Give them away.

With every exchange, touch both the pain and deficiencies in the world and your own joy and abilities. Take the pain and send your joy.

Does this practice lead to happiness? Not at all, but it does help you to understand the suffering and the struggles of others. Whatever ups and downs and joys and pains they encounter, you can be present with them because you know life is not perfect and you do not expect it to be.

As my teacher once said, "If you could really take away the suffering of everyone in the world, taking all of it into you with a single breath, would you hesitate?"

Even if someone, driven by desperate want,
Steals or makes someone else steal everything you own,
Dedicate to him your body, your wealth and
All the good you have ever done or will do—this is the
      practice of a bodhisattva.

THIS IS THE FIRST OF SIX VERSES IN WHICH TOKMÉ Zongpo describes how to practice in the face of injury, insult or the incomprehensible — situations that commonly provoke anger and rage. In all these situations you use anger as a basis for taking and sending practice.

You arrive home and step out of your car. Something does not feel right. Your front door is open. Cautiously you go in. The living room is a mess, your computer and television gone. You go to your bedroom. It has been ripped apart, drawers pulled open and clothes everywhere. The safe where you keep your valuables is gone and so is your jewelry.

You have been robbed.

You don't feel safe anymore. Your own home feels like a strange and hostile environment. You do not know who or what to trust. And you are angry—angry at the thief who broke into your home, angry at yourself for not taking more precautions, angry at a world in which people steal. You want the thief caught and punished. You want him to know what it feels like to be robbed. You want him to know what it is like to be frightened and scared.

You change the locks and install a security system. You have an expert find the weak points in your home and fix them. You know you have made it much harder for another thief to break in, yet you cannot sleep at night. You are still angry, outraged and resentful. You feel you have lost something else, a sense of security, and you do not know how to get it back.

Culture and society seduce you into a misleading way of thinking, that the cars, furniture, clothes and money that you own are actually yours. The robbery shattered that illusion. It is a painful learning, no doubt, but the theft has opened your eyes, and you see now that what you own is not actually yours. You have the use of your possessions, but they can be taken from you at any time.

What do you do?

You can, of course, continue to be consumed by anger and outrage and continue to lose sleep. Or you can use this theft to cultivate compassion, dismantle the spell of ownership and wake up a little.

Begin with your pain and upset. You have been violated, physically and emotionally. That is a fact. You cannot gloss it over. Open to the pain in your body and in your heart. Explore how much you can experience before you tip over the edge and are lost in feelings of anger, fear and violation. It is not helpful to let those feelings take over completely. Go to the edge of what you can experience and not be consumed, and rest right there.

Then turn attention to the person who robbed you. Touch how needy, desperate, angry or cold you would have to be in order to steal from someone else, by force or by cunning. Then mentally give to the other everything he or she needs to be free and at peace. Do this over and over again, touching and taking in that person's need, anger and hardness, touching and sending your good fortune and your care and regard for others.

What happens? You sense in your body what it is like to be so desperate, so cold or so ruthless. Taking those feelings in may be uncomfortable, but do it anyway. You may not want to send your wealth and good fortune, either. It is yours, after all. Send it anyway.

This is not a feel-good practice. Don't try to make it one. Just do it.

Then something shifts. Your experience of pain changes from being a threat to being a sensation. You do not make this change happen. It is not a decision on your part. It happens on its own. Something shifts inside you, and you experience your pain differently. You can now, in a different way, take in the pain of the thief who robbed you. It may be intense and unpleasant, but you can take it in. You can also take in the pain of others who have been robbed and the pain of all those who rob and steal. You understand how destructive and soul-destroying pain is, and you want everyone to be free of it.

You can also send your own wealth, enjoyment and appreciation of life freely to others. You can send your own generosity and openness, your respect for others and the joy of sharing and giving. You send all these with a free and open heart to both those who have been robbed and those who rob. Prejudice and judgment drop away and an unexpected joy opens up.

If you practice this long enough, you begin to see that it is all like a dream. You see how the stories you use to give your life structure—this is mine, that is yours, yours, mine, mine, yours—seduce you into an illusion, the illusion of ownership.

Nothing you own is truly yours. Your car is not yours. You just have the use of it as long you make the payments. If it is stolen, it is not yours anymore. Your home is not yours. You pay a mortgage, and that gives you the use of your home. The books in your home are not yours. If there is a flood, a fire or another theft, you no longer have the use of them. Even the money in your bank account is not yours. You just have the use of it. It can be taken from you by identify theft, bank errors, con artists, market fluctuations or inflation.

All that you have is what you experience right now. That, and only that, is yours. Everything else is an idea, a story, an interpretation, a dream. As you wake up to the understanding that all these notions about life are nothing but mist and smoke, you feel both a tremendous loss and a great relief. You also feel an infinite compassion for those who are caught in the dream and cannot see beyond it.

Even if you have done nothing wrong at all
And someone still tries to take your head off,
Spurred by compassion
Take all his or her venom into you—this is the practice of
    a bodhisattva.

YOUR PHONE RINGS. IT IS YOUR BOSS. WITHOUT ANY
warning she lays into you. She is so angry and upset you can hardly
understand her. Whatever it is, you are to blame—that much is
clear. She tells you what she has done and is going to do. Those
words come through loud and clear, but you cannot believe them.
When she is finished, she just hangs up.

You are in shock. You are speechless. You cannot believe what
just happened. You have just lost your job. And you did not do
anything!

"What did I do to deserve this?" you ask. You grasp for an
explanation—psychological, sociological, neurological, biological,
physiological, epistemological, ontological, astrological, mytho-
logical—any explanation, as long as it is logical.

Once the initial shock dissipates, emotional reactions start to
run. You feel cut off, alone, isolated, unloved and unappreciated.
You are angry, outraged, and you want to destroy anything and
everything within your reach.

The next moment you want to rise above it all—it is the universe telling you what you have to learn, it is the play of emptiness,
it is the dance of the cosmos. Then you plunge back into distress
and despair. One moment you are ready to settle for a self-satisfy-
ing dose of martyrdom, the next moment you coldly plot ways to
take down the whole company.

You are lost in reaction. What do you do?

Again, Tokmé Zongpo suggests taking and sending.

Take in the venom of anger, from her and from all beings. Send out understanding and love. Take in the pain of rejection and send out your joy of acceptance. Take in loss and fear and send out your wealth and confidence.

Still the stories run. "It isn't fair," you think. You reconstruct in your mind what likely happened, how you ended up being fired for something you did not do, but it is too late. The world has moved on. You are where you are and it is not fair. From all beings, everywhere, take in all the unfairness they encounter. Take in the lack of understanding and the pain, too, of those who are unfair, judgmental, critical and punitive. Send out equanimity, impartiality, patience and understanding.

What leads you to focus on fairness? As you practice and feel the part of you that wants justice and fairness, you may be surprised at how young it feels. It is often a child's wish, a child who has yet to come to terms with the unpredictable topsy-turvy chaos that is life.

Then it hits you. Your boss was really upset. She yelled at you like a child having a tantrum.

With this insight, your taking and sending practice changes. You see that her pain is pain in the same way your pain is pain, and you take her pain into yours, along with the pain of everyone who is hurt or confused by the unpredictable ways of the world. Send to them the warmth of your love, the gentle touch of your patience and the peace of your equanimity in the face of the inevitable inequities in life.

Drop any concern for justice and fairness. These are ideals, ideas that your patterns easily twist and shape to their own ends. Practice goes nowhere if you follow this path. You are soon lost in interpretation, conceptual thinking, unacknowledged prejudice and bias. Do not claim access to a higher truth, either, because you are then claiming the power and the right to decide for others.

Instead, turn your attention to your own hopes and dreams and bring them into your practice of taking and sending. Take in all the lost, broken and unlived dreams that people experience in their lives every day. Send to them all the success, enjoyment or accomplishment you have ever experienced.

Use taking and sending to open to the totality of pain and suffering in the world and take it in. Use it to open to the totality of joy and happiness in you and send it out.

Practice this until all thought and projection fall away and you are clear and awake in the experience of taking and sending.

Depending on circumstances, it may be possible to say something to your boss or do something to restore balance. Equally, there may be no possibility in saying or doing anything. You can know what to do only when you are no longer disturbed by your emotional reactions and you are free from the confusion of the conceptual mind.

This is the practice of a bodhisattva.

Even if someone broadcasts to the whole universe
Slanderous and ugly rumors about you,
Again and again, with an open and caring heart,
Praise his or her abilities—this is the practice of
    a bodhisattva.

THE RUMOR IS ALL OVER TOWN. EVERYONE IS TALKING
about it. People ask you again and again, "How could you do
that?" No matter how often you say, "I didn't," or "It wasn't like
that," the questions and censures keep coming. Your protests carry
little weight. Whatever you say, others twist and turn it against
you.

The rumor starts to spread on the internet. A popular blog
picks it up. People who have no connection with you and know
nothing about you comment on your supposedly abhorrent behavior. Another site picks it up, and then another.

Every time you hear about it, every time you read about it, you
feel as if you have been physically attacked. Your guts tighten up,
your chest hurts, you double over and you have trouble breathing. Anger, shock, incredulity, worry, fear and panic flood you.
You have become an icon of misbehavior, a symbol of what people
most hate and fear.

You know who is responsible. You know exactly how the rumor
started, but there is nothing you can do about it. The rumormon-
ger is impervious to your entreaties and seemingly intent on making as many people as possible see you in the worst possible light.

You do not want to go out. When you do, your only hope is that
no one recognizes you.

You feel victimized, violated, isolated, cut off from all ordinary human connection. You are angry and want to strike back, refuting the charges, defending your reputation and attacking the source of the rumors. You want revenge. You want justice. You want your life back. You want to retaliate, if only not to feel so helpless. But you do feel helpless.

Your every thought is centered on you.

You are concerned about the damage and the harm that these rumors are doing to those who know you, respect you or look up to you. Even then, it is still about you.

Start here. Every idea you have about you is not true. They are just ideas. Every idea others have about you is not true. They are just ideas. What happens? Perhaps you dropped open in an unexpected way. Now begin taking and sending.

Take in the pain of everyone who has felt the stabs of ugly rumors and bled from the slashes of false or misleading accusations. Send them your own experience of being respected and praised, loved and admired. Take in the pain of those who spread such rumors and seek to damage the reputations of others. Take in the hurt, malevolence, anger or bitterness that drives them. Send to them, too, whatever you know from your own life that soothes the hurts, defuses the anger and releases the bitterness.

With every breath, go to the edge of what you can feel and still be present and aware of where you are, what you are experiencing and what you are doing. In taking in the pain, feel the bite of that pain, but do not lose yourself in it. In sending your experience of being appreciated and praised, send it even as you feel the tug of wanting to keep it for yourself.

Open and take in the pain that drives your attacker. Take it into your pain and hurt. Feel all of it as deeply as you can. In return, send your understanding and appreciation. Let it pour out of you like a river of moonlight, soothing, calming and healing everything it touches. As that river flows out of you, you, too, feel its touch and you are able to open more deeply to the pain that is present in you, your assailant, those who are hurt by slander and rumors and those who hurt others with slander and rumors.

As you do this, you see, too, how attached you are to your reputation. Take in the attachment and the pain of attachment. Take in the pride one feels from being well regarded, praised and admired. Send to everyone the high regard, praise and admiration you have received. Send them the joy you feel when you are praised.

Bit by bit you see that there is nothing in you to be attacked, slandered or victimized, and nothing to praised, respected or idolized. You see you are not your reputation. You do not own it. It does not belong to you. It is not you and it is not yours. It is a collection of thoughts and feelings in the minds of others about what you have done, what they have heard you have done and what they think you have done.

Something in you lets go. You realize that you cannot control the world. Now, from all beings, take in the pain of not being able to control your own life and send the joy of living without hope and fear.

In these ways, use taking and sending to experience every aspect of slander and being slandered, of praise and being praised. When you can experience everything, the good and the bad, there is nothing you need to grasp or oppose.

What happens in your heart now? Against the pain of the world, you are able to accept your own pain. Your heart goes out to others, to the person who slandered you, to everyone who slanders or has been slandered.

These understandings are not merely ideas. When you touch your own pain, and through that, the pain of the world, there really is no enemy. You simply cannot go there.

Many people just pay lip service to these instructions. They retreat into an idealization of what it means to be a bodhisattva. They use the behavioral codes to mask their own anger and hurt and do not let themselves feel the intensity of their own pain, let alone the pain of the world. That is understandable. It is often unthinkably frightening to experience what goes on inside you. If you wish to be free, however, you have no choice.

Even if someone humiliates you and denounces you
In front of a crowd of people,
Think of this person as your teacher
And humbly honor him—this is the practice of a bodhisattva.

"HOW COULD I DO THAT?" YOU ASK YOURSELF. YOU DO
not know, and you are utterly, miserably ashamed. You made a
mistake. You know you made a mistake and you are struggling to
come to terms with it. You have apologized. You did your best to
set things right but you still have to live with the consequences.
You also did your best to understand how you could make that
mistake and you are clear that it will never happen again. Now you
have put it aside and gone on with your life.

It does not always end there.

A few people discover what happened and are now taking you
to task publicly. They demand that you be held accountable.

"Why are they doing this?" you wonder. You have apologized.
You have done what you could to make things right. What business is it of theirs?

Their denunciations make you live your mistake over and over
again, hundreds and hundreds of times. Each time you recall a
crucial decision point, hot sticky sensations flash through your
body as you quiver and shake inside. A primal fear seizes your guts
and turns them inside out. You want to curl up in a dark corner,
throw up and let the world forget that you ever existed. In the next
moment you feel an urge to strike out at your assailants, lashing
them with ugly accounts of their own shortcomings, too. You feel
naked, exposed, invaded. Nothing is private.

You are in the grip of shame. Your attempt to put that part of you aside has failed. Your antagonists have put you directly in touch with what you tried to ignore.

Is that not exactly what your teacher does, put you in touch with those parts of you that you ignore? Most teachers do not use public humiliation or shame, but they do point out those places where you are not awake or aware. In doing so, they give you a chance to work with them.

Remembering that, move into taking and sending. Take in the pain that your mistake caused for others, not only from the people you hurt but also from everyone who has suffered similar pain. Send out your own good health, your good fortune and particularly whatever you know in your life that might ease their pain. Take in the pain of all those who make similar mistakes and send them your understanding, patience and care. Take in the anger and pain from those who have humiliated you and send them your gratitude and appreciation for bringing attention to what you had put aside and forgotten.

Shame is tough. It catches you in a story of betrayal, self-betrayal, honor, guilt and taboos. You feel that you have violated a cosmic law, that you are no longer fit to be called a human being, that you are the lowest of the low, the vilest of the vile and that you will never be able to live this down. Anger flares up, again and again, to distract you from feeling like the vile and loathsome person you believe yourself to be.

You are obsessed with your identity, your sense of who you are.

In the context of Buddhist practice, this is all grist for the mill. Shame is seen as a source of virtue because it leads you to restrain your impulses and it shines a spotlight on your investment in how you see yourself and how others see you.

As you practice, keep an open field of attention by including not only your body, but also the whole world and the whole universe in your awareness. Do taking and sending with everyone. At the same time, include the part of you that you tried to ignore. Do not focus on it. Just keep it in awareness. You may experience it in different ways—as a small hard knot, as a pervasive physical agitation, as pain, physical, emotional or both, as a haunting feeling at the edge of your awareness. You do not need to do anything with it. From time to time, incorporate it into your taking and sending, taking in its pain and giving it your joy and well-being, just as you do with everyone.

At some point, a shift takes place—something in you crumbles and falls apart. You see that the humiliation you feel is exactly the same as the humiliation others feel, and the humiliation they feel is exactly the same as the humiliation you feel. All the stories about them and you vanish. You can now more freely take in the pain of humiliation and send out the joy of humility. Your mind and body are at peace. The pain is still there, but, strangely, you feel whole and complete and, at the same time, like nothing at all.

And then it strikes you. Without that public humiliation, without all that shame, you would not have come to this understanding and acceptance—the patterns in you were so deep, the holding so strong. Those people who denounced you, who left you no place to hide really are like your teacher. In a strange way, you are grateful to them, and your anger evaporates.

While you may be able to make use of shame this way, it does not follow that shame is always good for you. It depends on context and it depends on you.

In the context of a group, shame serves to preserve the cohesion of a group or society. It is the basis for the ethic of honor, an ethic that works to restrain antisocial behavior. Taken too far, it gives rise to antisocial and even inhumane behavior. In duels, for instance, one is just defending pride. "Honor" killings, in which a father or brother kills a daughter or sister who has been raped, are obviously inhumane.

Shame in this context is about belonging or not belonging to a group. You have a choice to make: conform to social or peer expectations or live your own values, wherever they lead.

Another unhealthy form of shame is an insistent relentless self-blaming. It is there even when neither personal nor social codes have been violated. It is based on a resilient negative identity that formed as a survival mechanism when you were abused or were unable to stop something terrible from happening. This form of shame is consistently accompanied by feelings of hopelessness and despair.

You can, if you are careful, use meditation practice to touch the core emotional reactions that led to the formation of this negative identity. However, because such internalized shame often forms through a relationship, it may be that a different experience of relationship, one of loving kindness, is needed for the negative identity to let go.

When you encounter shame, take a moment to see which of these three forms is operating. It is possible that all three are present. In that situation, you have to carefully pick them apart, working with taking and sending for the one, being clear about your relationship with a group for the second, and doing what is necessary to undo the third.

Even if a person you have cared for as your own child
Treats you as her worst enemy,
Lavish her with loving attention
Like a mother caring for her ill child—this is the practice of
a bodhisattva.

YOU CANNOT BELIEVE YOUR EYES. THIS CHILD THAT
you took care of since she was born, who once gazed at you with
love and joy, now glowers at you, her eyes stony and cold.

Your stomach knots up and you gasp for breath. You feel as if
a knife has cut into your heart or a dagger has plunged into your
back. You arch in pain, your back breaking as it bends horribly in
the wrong direction.

Except for the loss of a child, perhaps the greatest pain a parent
can know is the pain that arises when her child turns on her and
sees her as an enemy. As Shakespeare's King Lear laments:

How sharper than a serpent's tooth it is
To have a thankless child!

If you have ever nurtured, nourished, guided, taught, or mentored someone who later turned on you, you know something of
this pain.

Kindness given is not always returned. When it comes back
as anger, aggression or betrayal, it is like a physical blow. Your
heart cracks as waves of disbelief wash through you. Other feelings
slowly register—denial, anger, despair, hurt...

Forget about how life should unfold. Forget about how grateful your child, student, client or patient should be. A sense of a natural order is part of your biological makeup. Family, friends, society and culture have all reinforced it. You believe in it. Such ideas are expressions of a belief, an idea, about the world.

Instead, relate to the pain that is clearly there. Be awake in and to what is happening. Take in the pain that she is feeling. Take it into the pain you are feeling. Take in her anger. Take it into your anger. Feel your anger, and any hurt, pain or sadness associated with it, and take in the anger of all beings everywhere. Send out the love and care you have given in the past. Send it out again and again. Send it out magnified a hundred, a thousand, a million times. Open your heart to everyone who is hurt, angry or confused and take in all their suffering, whatever form it takes. Send out your care, your love, your well-being and understanding. Give everything away.

Wake up from the sleep of belief, even such a deep-seated belief as the natural order of life. Wake up to the fact that there is, in the end, nothing you can count on, nothing on which you can rely, nothing in which you can trust. Far from being a negative, this clarity, this absence of any absolute reference, is freedom—nothing around you, outside you or inside you can define in absolute terms who or what you are. You are what you are, and life is what it is. You, just as you are right now, have the potential to experience whatever life throws at you, even the ingratitude of your child. Rest in that clarity and continue to practice taking and sending, mixing awareness with your life and letting go of ideas, beliefs, stories or agendas.

Anger can then be understood as an expression of a natural intelligence telling you that a line has been crossed. Her anger points to a line in her. Your anger points to a line in you. You may not know the line in her. You may not even know the line in you, but those lines are there.

When you practice this way, your actions are not dictated by anger, whether as persecutor or victim. You may reset a boundary.

You may extend a helping hand. You may do nothing. Whatever you do, your action comes from clarity—from meeting and embracing the totality of your experience, internal and external. Here, compassion is not a method or a means to an end but a result, the result of being awake and present with the pain in you, in the other and in the world.

If you feel a compulsion to express your care and concern, be careful. Unwanted attention can also cross a line. Do just what needs to be done—no more and no less.

Even if your peers or those below you
Put you down to make themselves look better,
Treat them respectfully as if they were your teacher:
Put them above you—this is the practice of a bodhisattva.

SUPPOSE YOU ARE PART OF A GROUP WORKING ON A project. Something has gone wrong, and all of you are trying to understand what happened and what to do next. People in the group come up with different ideas as to what to do. Tensions rise as competing interests come to the surface. You put forward an idea that you think will work for everyone. A colleague dismisses your suggestion with a witty comment at your expense. You are a little stunned and say nothing. He then floats his own idea, which is only slightly different from yours. Because you have been sidelined, the group quickly supports his idea. You are left looking stupid, incompetent and out of touch.

When someone puts you down, usually the person you are most concerned about is you. Life comes at you like a herd of wild horses. You may dodge one way or another to avoid being trampled. You may look for a chance to grab the mane of a horse so you can haul yourself up and ride away. Whatever you do, your main concern is you.

Open to what has just happened. Someone put you down and sidelined you, and you are upset, angry and offended. Your tormenter has brought out a reactive pattern in you and brought it out so vividly that you cannot ignore it. It jolts you awake. You are attached, very attached, to what people think of you and how people regard you. Once you see that clearly, resentment, anger and embarrassment start to fall away. You may even laugh or sigh inside. You were caught — once again. Your tormentor has functioned as a teacher.

However you feel about being put down, use that feeling for taking and sending. If you are angry, take in the anger of others and send them whatever joy and peace of mind you have known in your life. If you are resentful, take in others' feelings of resentment and send respect and appreciation. If you are offended, take in the pain and insult and send praise and honor. If you are confused, take in confusion and send clarity and insight. Take in the pain of being put down and send out the warmth of courtesy and encouragement. Take in the emotional reactions that drive one person to put down another and send out your ability to treat everyone, even your worst enemy, with kindness and respect.

From there, it is more possible to disengage from the gameplaying and one-upmanship so common in life, to treat your assailant with respect and consideration and to focus on what needs to be done.

All through this section Tokmé Zongpo has described how to use unpleasant and painful situations to deepen practice. He means business. His instructions are not pragmatic strategies for managing difficult situations. They are ways to deepen your relationship with life itself by moving into the clear natural awareness that is the essence of human experience.

You cannot know what to do in any situation as long as you are in the grip of a reaction. Reactions distort your perception and limit the range of possible responses. You cannot see clearly. You cannot make decisions clearly. Nor can you speak or act clearly. Those possibilities begin to open up only when you are aware that you are in reaction. Awareness is key.

Reactions run deep. Beliefs are reactions solidified into a worldview that cannot be questioned. Belief marks the line at which your ability to think rationally stops. Emotions such as pride, jealousy or greed are reactions that are activated whenever fundamental beliefs, including the belief that you exist as a separate entity, are threatened. These emotions influence what you see, how you see and how you evaluate what you see—always in service of a conditioned sense of self. Many physical gestures and movements are automatic reactions, often biologically conditioned, that give expression to those emotions and give them power. Thoughts and stories are largely reactions, movements in your mind that function to dissipate attention and dull the awareness that just knows.

The purpose of taking and sending is to use difficult and powerful emotional reactions to awaken into a clear awareness free from the projections of thought and feeling. For this transformation to take place (again, this is not something you do, it is something that happens), attention has to be at a level of energy higher than the emotional reactions that arise in you. To access that level of energy, you draw on your commitment to compassion as it is expressed in the bodhisattva ideal and practiced in taking and sending.

When you are down and out, held in contempt,
Desperately ill and emotionally crazed,
Don't lose heart. Take into you
The suffering and negativity of all beings—this is the
    practice of a bodhisattva.

YOU BELIEVE THAT PRACTICE WILL MAKE YOUR LIFE
better, or at least less painful. Would that this were true!

At any moment you could lose your partner, child, parent or
close friend through accident, flood, earthquake or violence. A fall,
a stroke, a genetic defect or an unknown pollutant can suddenly
leave you disabled or disfigured. Your work, your livelihood, can
vanish with the flick of a pen.

Do you think your practice can prevent any of these from
happening?

Be honest. Anything can drive you crazy: a selfish sibling, a car
that does not start, an unexpected traffic jam, an overbearing boss,
a blank screen on your computer, a hormonal imbalance... It does
not take much.

Adversity is part of life. You cannot predict it. You cannot prevent it. You cannot control it.

When you feel that your life is hopelessly bad and you cannot
see how it is going to improve, can you sit in your misery and wish
that through your suffering and struggles all sentient beings are
freed from theirs?

Recall a time when bad luck, misfortune or mere inconvenience upset you. Let it build until you feel how upset you were.
Take a breath, pause for a moment, and then say, "I'm totally

miserable, destitute, confused and unhappy and I cannot do anything about it. Still, with all my heart, I wish that the suffering of all who encounter anything similar comes into me and that they are free of it." As you breathe in, take everyone else's struggles and suffering into you. When you breathe out, recall any vestige of joy from another time in your life and send it out to everyone. Waves of resistance may flood your body, but make the exchange anyway, over and over again, coordinating it with your breath.

At some point—in a few minutes, in a few days, in a few years, no one can say when—something changes. What changes is not your situation, nor your pain, nor your misery, nor your confusion. You just stop struggling against them, and that makes all the difference.

Something unknown and unnamable lets go. A door opens. In your pain and confusion you find a clear open awareness. That awareness is not different from your pain and confusion. The pain and confusion are not different from the awareness. There is not one or the other, nor is there one without the other, and you can rest in the awareness as you experience the pain.

You understand that you are experiencing what everyone else experiences: the vexations, annoyances, aggravations and tragedies of the human condition. You see that no one, not you, nor anyone else, can control or even predict what happens in life. You see the futility of blame, rage, judgment or self-pity.

Compassion—the understanding and acceptance of the pain of the world—arises naturally. You sit there, heart broken in one way, at peace in another.

There are many ways to meet adversity, but the practice of taking and sending is one of the simplest and most powerful.

Even when you are famous, honored by all
And as rich as the god of wealth himself,
Know that success in the world is ephemeral
And don't let it go to your head—this is the practice of
    a bodhisattva.

ACCORDING TO NIETZSCHE, WHAT DOES NOT KILL you strengthens you. It is true. Adversity does wake you up. You have to find a way to meet it, one way or another. If you need to, you develop new abilities. If you cannot change the external situation, you look inside. In either case, you bring more attention to your life, and you may even work through a pattern or two.

Good fortune, however, can put you to sleep. Your life becomes easier. Your survival is not threatened. Your immediate needs are met. You relax. You are in a good position—good for patterns to run.

When fortune smiles on you, you see it as evidence that you made the right decisions in your life. It is concrete proof that you are a superior person. Subtly or not so subtly, the way you relate to others changes. You adopt an air of entitlement and privilege and you expect others to treat you with the respect and deference you feel you deserve.

With good fortune your attitude to change also changes. Life is good. You want to keep it that way. You seek ways to make your wealth, reputation and status more secure. You take fewer risks. You become more conservative, concerned with the maintenance of the status quo and resistant to ideas and developments that could threaten your good fortune.

Why do you take credit for your good fortune? Much of it is a matter of pure luck. Where you were born, who your parents are and the opportunities you have or do not have in your life—most of it just luck. You exercise regularly and watch your diet, but your health depends just as much on your genes. Why do you take all the credit? You have a great job. Did you earn it, or did you happen to be in the right place at the right time? And if you win the lottery, why do you secretly congratulate yourself on picking just those numbers?

If you take credit for all the good in your life, why do you not take equal credit for the accidents and mistakes?

Do not let prosperity and success fool you into thinking that you can avoid change. Natural disasters, economic downturns, a new government, changes in technology, illness, war—anything—can wipe out your good fortune in a moment. It can be here one day and gone the next. As Tokmé Zongpo writes in verse nine:

The happiness of the three worlds disappears in a moment,
Like a dewdrop on a blade of grass.

How do you use good fortune to wake up in your life? What can you do so that you do not go to sleep?

Recall an occasion when something good happened in your life. Your boyfriend proposed to you. You found the job you always wanted. You made a winning play in a crucial game. Your spouse recovered from a life-threatening illness. You received an unexpected windfall.

Feel what happens in your body when you recall such experiences. If your body is suffused with warmth and ease, send that warmth and ease, along with your good fortune, to all beings everywhere. Take in the difficulties, pain and troubles in their lives. If you feel tense and on edge, take in the same discomfort from all beings and send them your wealth, good fortune and comfort.

Do the same with the emotions that arise. Send happiness,

joy, relief and peace to all beings. Take in anxiety, uncertainty and need. If you feel numb and lifeless, take the same feelings from others and send them your own vitality and enjoyment of sights, sounds, tastes, touches and aromas.

Do the same with the stories. Send them the pat on the back you give yourself when everything is going well in your life. Take in blame and shame from all beings. Take in pride and smug satisfaction. Send them joy, appreciation and humility. Send them the opportunities you have to do good and help others. Take in their struggles just to make ends meet. If you tell yourself you are unworthy and undeserving, take in those same thoughts from all beings. Send them praise, encouragement and confidence.

Open to everything—the sensations in your body, the feelings and the stories. Experience them all and use them as a basis for taking and sending.

From time to time ask, "Who experiences this good fortune?" As soon as you pose this question, something shifts. Whether your body was relaxed or agitated, it settles in a different way. Whatever emotions you were feeling lose their hold, as do the stories. Look and look again at what experiences good fortune. Do not try to figure it out. Just look. At some point, you see that there is nothing there, just the experience of good fortune and an awareness that knows it—the two not different, yet not the same. Rest right there.

Now look at the good fortune itself. What is it? If you look deeply, you see that success and good fortune are not solid entities. They are experiences that, like adversity and difficulty, arise and disappear in a nameless ineffable awareness, an awareness that has nothing to do with success and failure, prosperity or poverty, good fortune or bad.

Feelings of excitement and being special give way to a well of quiet joy and deep appreciation. If you nurture that joy and appreciation, your good fortune cannot lull you into the sleep of inattention, complacency and pride.

If you don't subdue the enemy inside—your own anger—
The more enemies you subdue outside, the more that come.
Muster the forces of loving kindness and compassion,
And subdue your own mind—this is the practice of
    a bodhisattva.

TOKMÉ ZONGPO TALKS ABOUT ANGER, YET HE USES the language of war—enemy, subdue, muster, forces. Is he saying you should wage a war against anger? Or is he speaking metaphorically?

Forget metaphors for a moment. If you do not resolve your own anger, you experience the world in terms of opposition and conflict, because that is how anger presents the world to you. No matter how many people you frighten, intimidate, lay into or beat up, all it takes is another disagreement, another vexation, and you are fighting again.

Now back to metaphors. You are a ball of fire, a red-hot iron rod, a vat of molten copper. Anyone who comes near you feels the heat. If they miss their cue or make the slightest mistake, fire roars from your mouth and engulfs them in flames. The more people you incinerate, the more alone you are. The more alone you are, the more sensitive you are and the more people you incinerate. The pattern just keeps going around and around.

Welcome to hell—one of the hot hells, to be precise.

If you take Tokmé Zongpo's advice literally, you are going to stay in hell. When you wage war on anger, even with the forces of loving kindness and compassion, you are still waging war. A war on hell means you are in hell. War is not the way out.

In Buddhist practice, there are basically three ways to work with anger or other strong reactive emotions: dissolve, employ or transform.

To dissolve anger, experience it. Experience it without expressing it or repressing it.

To return to the language of metaphor, your anger is a frightened, scared, hurt and lonely child having a tantrum. Hold that child tenderly in your attention. The tenderness is where the "forces" of loving kindness and compassion come in. Do not try to make her do anything. Just hold her. Let her cry. Let her rage. Do not react to her pain, distress, fear or outbursts. Hold her tenderly with loving kindness and compassion.

Loving kindness opens you to her rage. You do not reject it. You do not try to make it go away. Compassion enables you to be present with her pain. You do not try to fix it. You do not try to make it go away. You cannot make it go away, of course, but you can be there with it.

Sit there and experience all the anger, pain, hurt and confusion in you. That is your practice—to experience it without getting lost in it. Little by little, that child feels your quiet presence. Little by little, she calms down. At some point, an understanding arises, an insight into the anger, hurt and confusion you are feeling and the whole reactive cycle dissolves.

To employ anger, practice taking and sending. Take in the anger of everyone in the world—rage, hatred, irritation, resentment and fury. Take in their hurt, pain, confusion and sadness. Send them all the joy, happiness, peace and contentment you have known and ever will know. Use your own anger to move into this exchange with others. The friction between your self-centered anger and your other-centered wish to help generates energy. As you open to both your anger and the pain of the human condition, your own anger cannot hold and it collapses.

To transform anger, open completely to the experience of anger—all the physical sensations, all the emotions, all the stories—and then ask, "What experiences all this?" When you ask that question, a shift takes place. You look and you see nothing. Rest right there and look. Look in the resting. Rest in the looking. At some point, the energy of anger arises as clarity, as a mirror-like timeless awareness. This is not something you make happen. When you have the capacity to experience your anger and to rest in looking at it, this transformation just happens. It is not something you do.

This last approach sounds like an easy shortcut, but it requires a high level of attention—a stability and clarity that allow you to rest and look even when you are a flaming ball of rage.

If you set loving kindness and compassion against anger, if you try to oppose anger with either of these, anger always wins. The use of "forces" here refers not to opposition, but to the depth and power of your loving kindness and compassion—you can experience your anger, all of it, without suppressing or expressing it.

Anger is a reactive mechanism that generates energy to deal with threats to your survival. When you approach anger itself as a threat that has to be eliminated, you trigger exactly that mechanism. The more you oppose anger, even with loving kindness or compassion, the more strongly the survival reaction runs. You may behave as if you are compassionate, but the unresolved anger smolders inside, whether you are aware of it or not. It leaks out in ways you do not notice and it can flare up at any time.

Practice is a puzzle. You practice to make things better, but for things to change for the better, you have to let go of wanting them to be better. You have probably heard this before, but it is important: do the practice, but do not do it with the hope that you will make something happen. Just do it.

Sensual pleasures are like salty water:
The deeper you drink, the thirstier you become.
Any object you attach to,
Right away, let it go—this is the practice of a bodhisattva.

"JUST ONE MORE POTATO CHIP," YOU SAY, BUT YOU always want another. After all, they are designed to make you want more.

Soon enough the whole bag of potato chips is gone, and you still want more. Nothing satisfies. You always want another cup of coffee, another kiss, another car, another silk dress, another this, another that.

Taste, smell, touch, sight, sound—you seek stimulating, engaging, entrancing, enthralling, erotic, heart-stopping, mind-blowing sensations. Are you ever satisfied? Can you ever be satisfied?

The problem is not your enjoyment, enjoying the chocolate, the silk or the feel of your lover's skin. The problem is not the object of your enjoyment, either. The problem is that you make that one feeling of satisfaction your whole world and then try to stay there. But the sensation passes and the satisfaction fades. You want to hold onto the satisfaction or feel it again and again. When you cannot, you feel uneasy, anxious and incomplete. You crave the sensation and how it makes you feel.

In the pursuit of freedom, some people try to solve this problem by going to the opposite extreme. They avoid all sensory pleasure. Asceticism has a long tradition, and it is a way to build discipline, to develop capacity or to discover possibilities that you did not know were in you. To take asceticism as an end in itself is a denial of life. Body, mind and heart simply wither.

One of Buddha's great insights was that both denial and indulgence are dead ends.

Desire triggers the sensations of hunger and thirst. When you notice that, stop right there. These sensations—sometimes physical, sometimes emotional, sometimes both—set off biological mechanisms that cause your attention to collapse. Desire takes over, desire for anything that eases the hunger and slakes the thirst.

Instead, open to everything in your experience including the hunger and thirst of desire. Open to everything you see, all at once. Then include everything you hear, all at the same time. Then include all the kinesthetic and tactile sensations in your body, all the muscular contractions and tension, again, all at the same time. Now include all the internal sensations, reactions, emotions, thoughts, stories, and memories. Include the hunger and thirst, the desire, along with everything else. Then rest in all of it.

What happens to your desire? It becomes simply one of a number of movements in your field of experience. You experience it along with everything else. What experiences desire? That, too, is simply one of a number of movements in your field of experience. Is it you? Your mind stops and a space opens.

Look at the object of your desire again. How do you experience it now? If it is a flower, say, you notice all the details. If it is your lover, you see the contours of her face, the subtle changes in hues, the way her hair falls, the way she breathes. And you appreciate her in a whole new way because now you see her without being driven by desire.

Whatever arises in experience is your own mind.
Mind itself is free of any conceptual limitations.
Know that and don't entertain
Subject-object fixations—this is the practice of a bodhisattva.

TAKE A BREATH. LET IT OUT SLOWLY—WITHOUT STRAIN.
Do that again three or more times until mind and body settle
naturally.

Think of something. It can be anything, but think of just one
thing—your partner, a friend, a flower or an idea. The thought can
be a word or phrase, a picture or a sound.

Where is that thought? In your mind, of course, but what does
that mean? Is the thought inside your head? Is it outside your
head?

It is there. It is vivid. Say you have a picture in your mind.
Where is that picture—inside, outside, where?

If you have not done this exercise before, by now you are probably flooded with thoughts and ideas and are trying to figure out
how to do it. Instead, let it all go and start again.

Go back to the three breaths and let mind and body settle. Now
think a thought about just one thing. Picture it, if you wish. Where
is that picture?

When you look this time, do not look with your mind. Do not
look with your eyes. Do not try to figure anything out. Just look—
with your whole being, including your body.

You know, see or hear the thought. The thought is there, definitely, but where is it?

Do not try to figure this out. Just look. Where is it?
You cannot say.

Just rest there. You cannot say, so do not try to say. Just rest there, resting and looking.

Now take a feeling—anger, love, joy, grief, pride, compassion—it does not matter which. Bring the feeling to mind and ask, "Where is it?"

As for the physical sensations associated with those feelings, we will deal with those in a moment. For now, just ask, "Where is the feeling?" and look. What do you see?

You feel the anger. You feel the love. You feel the physical sensations. But where is the feeling? You say, "In my mind," but where is that?

You can feel the physical sensations—tension, contraction, and tightness with anger and warmth, relaxation and possibly a different kind of tension, with love. Are the physical sensations the feeling? There is an emotional quality, too. Where is that?

You cannot say. No one can. Again, rest there, looking and resting.

Now look at an object—a chair, this book, a vase, anything that you can look at right now. You see the object. But where is the seeing? Where does the seeing take place?

You may think, "In my head!" But is the seeing in your head? If you look at an object that is larger than your head, it is hard to see how the seeing could take place in your head.

"It takes place in my mind," you say. Exactly, but where is that? You cannot say.

And you are right back where you were with thoughts and feelings. They are there, but you cannot say where they are. You see, but you cannot say where the seeing is.

It is the same with the other senses, but the habituations with some of them are stronger. Try sound first. Listen to a piece of music, the ringing of a bell or the hum of your refrigerator. Where is the hearing?

You cannot say.

It is the same with physical sensations. You feel them. You associate them with very specific parts of your body, an itch on your back, the texture of your shirt, the tightness in your jaw when you are angry, the pain in a stiff muscle, a queasy feeling in your stomach when you are uncomfortable with a question. But where does the sensing take place?

You cannot say.

Remember what Tokmé Zongpo says: whatever arises in experience is your own mind.

In other words, what you experience is your mind. Your mind is not a thing. It is not located anywhere. Your mind is what you experience. What you experience is your mind.

Wherever you are as you read this, look around, open to everything that you see, everything that you hear or touch, everything that you think and feel.

All those experiences—the seeing, the hearing, the feeling, the thinking—all that is your mind.

It is a bit like a dream.

Rest there for a few moments, taking it all in, a little puzzled, perhaps a little in awe.

It is a different way of experiencing life.

What experiences all this? Again, do not try to figure this out. Do not start thinking about the question. Just ask the question and look. What experiences all this? Just look. Look in the resting. Rest in the looking.

It is a bit difficult at first, and stability in attention is very important here, but after a while, you become aware of a knowing, an awareness, that has nothing to do with thinking. It is clear, like water. Thoughts and feelings arise on their own. It is a bit like a mirror—you do not see the mirror itself, you just see the reflections in it. Mind is like that. Thoughts, feelings and sensory sensations arise without restriction. Yet, when you look for the mind itself, there is nothing there.

Rest again, looking in the resting, resting in the looking, resting in that awareness. Thoughts and feelings may come and go, but there is no observer, no watcher. They are there, and then they are gone, like snowflakes on a hot stone. It does not matter whether the thoughts are of "I" or some object. It does not matter whether they are explicit words or images or vague feelings and sensations. They are all movements in awareness, yet there is nothing there that moves.

This is not something you think. This is something you experience.

Most people are able to do this practice for only a moment or two before their attention destabilizes and they fall back into thinking, into the ordinary subject-object mode of experience. If that happens to you, do not try to hold on to shifts or insights. When attention crumbles, it crumbles. It is gone. Start again at the beginning, letting mind and body settle. Work at this patiently — quietly building capacity rather than trying to understand something or trying to make something happen or hold on to something that did happen.

In time you are able to rest for longer periods without your attention going to pieces. You can look more deeply and see more clearly. When you are able to rest in clear empty awareness, you can start learning how to live there. Begin with simple movements, then simple repetitive tasks, gradually include more sensations and work up to moving through your day. There will be lapses, of course, but that is why it is called practice.

When you come across something you enjoy,
Though beautiful to experience, like a summer rainbow,
Don't take it as real.
Let go of attachment—this is the practice of a bodhisattva.

THE LAST HUNDRED FEET ALMOST KILLED YOU, BUT you made it to the top of the pass. Tired but exhilarated, you sit down on a rock and take in the view. Below you, a long alpine meadow stretches into the distance, green with mountain grasses and dotted with pink, yellow and blue. A silvery ribbon weaves back and forth, light flashing from the sweeping curves. The deep green of old-growth forest on either side slopes up into hills and mountains that rise on the other side of the valley, the snow on their peaks shimmering in the distant blue. To your left water cascades over a ledge, the waterfall disintegrating into a thick mist dancing with rainbows in the afternoon sun. You look up into a clear blue sky, so clear and blue you lose yourself in its depths.

You have never felt so alive, so full of energy, so at peace. Don't take this as real?

You listen to a concert, and the beauty of the music brings tears to your eyes. Don't take this as real?

You watch your child and a friend playing together—and their laughter brings joy to your heart. Don't take this as real?

Does the word itself trip you up? It has a lot of meanings. On the one hand, everything you experience is real—if only because you experience it. On the other, nothing is real—because you cannot pin down anything you experience and say exactly what it is. This is one of the great paradoxes of the human condition. The challenge is to live in the paradox, in the mystery.

Take any of the examples above, or take one of your own, a moment when a work of art, a landscape, the company of a friend or a rich red wine by a warm fire, filled you with happiness and joy. At that moment you feel complete, full, at one with the world. Rest there, feeling that fullness, relaxed and open.

Now feel what happens when that moment passes. You start down the trail. You turn away from the painting to go to a meeting. You say goodbye to your friend. The wine glass is empty and the fire has died down. That feeling of completeness fades and longing arises. You think about the view, you recall the painting, you remember your friend, you savor the last flavors on your tongue, but it is not the same. You feel less complete, less full of life, less one with the world.

Your attention collapses down to the memory, to the object. You want to bring it back, hold onto it and keep it a little longer. You want that person, that landscape or that painting back in your life. You do not feel complete without it. You are complete, but you do not feel that way because you are no longer experiencing the whole. You are not including the change that has taken place in your feelings and your awareness. You close down to what you are experiencing right now because your attention is absorbed by what was instead of opening to what is.

What happens when you include the feelings of incompleteness and the longing that accompanies it?

Recall the landscape, your friend or the painting. Let yourself feel the longing in your heart and the way it arises in your body —the holding and the hoping—all at the same time. Sensations, feelings and thoughts arise and dissolve in the space of mind, like rainbows in the sky. Let them be there, visceral, sensual, ecstatic. If you wish, pose the question, "What knows all this?"

The way that you experience the tug of the longing changes. Both the longing and the tug become sensations, physical and emotional. At the same time, you experience a stillness inside, a quiet deep feeling that does not depend on anything. And the memory? You just appreciate and enjoy it, without being disturbed by the longing.

What does it mean to let something go? It means to let it be.

All forms of suffering are like dreaming that your child
      has died.
Taking confusion as real wears you out.
When you run into misfortune,
Look at it as confusion—this is the practice of a bodhisattva.

YOUR DAUGHTER HAS DIED. YOU CANNOT SPEAK. YOU
cannot think. Words utterly fail to touch your loss, your heart-
break, your grief or your pain. You sit on your couch, dumb and
deaf. Your home feels like an alien world. The natural order has
been horribly violated. You cannot understand how life can be so
cruel, so heartless, so unfeeling. Your closest friends come over,
but they are ghosts drifting through your home, their consoling
words faint echoes from another world. You are utterly alone in
your anguish.

And then you wake up.

Your heart is pounding. You rush to your daughter's room,
your heart in your mouth. There she is, sleeping peacefully, moonlight caressing her face. Tears of joy come to your eyes. A little
bewildered, a little stunned, you stumble back to your bed and sit
down.

It was a dream. It was just a dream.

But the feelings were so real!

A car accident, the loss of your job, a financial setback, an unexpected medical condition, these and other forms of misfortune
and adversity stir up powerful feelings and powerful stories, so

powerful that they often just take over, and you are, in effect, living in a dream.

That is the confusion.

Your first impulse is to push away the problem, the misfortune. Ignore it! Shut it out! Maybe it will just go away on its own. When that does not work, you go to war, blaming others, blaming yourself, seeking revenge, seeking justice or fairness. You go on a crusade, and your efforts may make the world a better place for others. But your own loss is still there, along with the pain and grief.

You cannot acknowledge it. You cannot face it. You organize your whole life to keep it at bay. You eat. You exercise. You work as hard as you can. But a part of your life has been cut out. It makes no difference what you do, you never feel whole, you never feel complete and you are never at peace.

Whether wanted or unwanted, pleasant or unpleasant, anticipated or unanticipated, everything you experience is your life, just as in a dream everything you experience is the dream.

When you encounter difficulties, the feelings and stories that arise in reaction are just that, feelings and stories. They are whirlwinds of confusion, based not in what is happening now but in deeply held beliefs about you and your relationship to the world. Let them swirl—leaves in the wind. Sometimes you fall back into them and lose touch with the present, but a moment of recognition always comes. Right then, come back to your body, come back to your breath, and rest. The confusion, the stories and the feelings are still there. They continue to swirl, but you are not lost in them.

Just rest. Do not try to control your feelings. Open to all the stories and feelings as much as you can without being consumed by them. You will experience shock, disorientation, anger and self-blaming—reactive mechanisms that protect you from the full impact of what has happened. Sit patiently and let your system sort itself out.

As you rest in the confusion, bit by bit, you separate your confusion from the challenge you are facing. Still, the impulse is to oppose. Ask yourself, "What am I opposing?" Then, "Do I need to oppose this?" And, finally, "Is opposing called for at all?"

When you no longer oppose what is happening in you, you are able to rest and see more clearly. What do you see? Look in the resting. Rest in the looking. In doing this, you are mixing awareness with what you experience and what you experience with awareness. Keep coming back to the clarity without losing the stability. Keep coming back to the stability without losing the clarity.

Learn to trust that clarity. Over time it enables you to act without relying on conceptual thinking or strategizing.

If those who want to be awake have to give even their bodies,
What need is there to talk about things that you simply own?
Be generous without looking
For any return or result—this is the practice of a bodhisattva.

IMAGINE YOU COME ACROSS A TIGRESS SO WEAK SHE
is unable to suckle her cubs. Moved by her plight, you lie down in
front of her, but she is too weak to kill you. You cut your arm with
your own knife and let your blood drip into her mouth. When she
has enough strength, she kills and eats you.

Arguably the best known of the tales of Buddha's former lives,
this story leaves the modern reader perplexed, if not horrified. Yet
the story puts you in touch, if only for a moment, with what it is
like to be free of all self-interest, right down to the level of basic
biology.

Just touch that freedom right now. What happens? Imagine
taking the echo of that touch into your life. What happens?

The story of Buddha and the tigress is an awful story, a terrible story. It is a terrible story because it leaves you terrified at the
possibility that to be truly human may take you far beyond your
own biological conditioning. It is an awful story because it fills
you with awe—bypassing your intellect and rational understanding and connecting you directly with a depth of compassion you
never considered.

What is generosity? It is giving. Period. It is giving without
strings, without reservations, without conditions. Something
moves from your hands to another's (figuratively or literally), and

in the process you let go of it, of how it is used and of what happens to it.

Any expectation of return, a reciprocation or a change in behavior means that you are not practicing generosity. You are trading, making a loan or manipulating.

How do you practice generosity?

Once a day, give something you own to someone else. You may give a paper clip or a flower, but the object has to be physical and it has to be yours. It may be expensive or inconsequential. It may be old or new. But it has to be yours. It has to be an actual object, too, so that you have the physical experience of giving, not just an imagined one.

Give one thing to someone once a day. That is the practice. Do not make a big deal of it, either. In other words, do not tell anyone that you are doing this practice.

Open to whatever arises in you when you give—hope of reciprocation, pride, wanting to be seen as generous, desire for control, expectation of thanks, sadness, joy in the giving, relief, loneliness, attachment to the gift, irritation with the exercise, etc. Let all the internal stuff that gets in the way of giving be there, along with all the physical and emotional sensations, stories and associations.

Do this every day, and see what happens over the course of weeks and months.

This verse is the first of six in which Tokmé Zongpo addresses each of the six perfections: generosity, ethical discipline, patience, energy, meditative stability and wisdom.

Perfection is a not a very good translation, but it is probably the best in English, and it is standard usage now. Neither the Sanskrit nor the Tibetan carries any notion of doing something perfectly. Instead, they point to a transcendent quality that is present when you act in complete clarity, when what you do is not mediated or distorted by the projections of reactive emotions and conceptual thinking.

How do you practice the perfection of generosity?

Every day, when you give your object, open to the whole experience and ask, "Who gives?" Do not answer the question. Do not think about it. Just ask the question.

You experience a shift. At first the shift lasts only a second or two. Keep doing this, once a day, every time you give. Bit by bit, the shift lasts a little longer. Rest there.

Over time, you notice that, whenever you give, you are a little more awake, a little more present. You do not think about giving. It just happens—no thinking, no self-consciousness, no pride, no attachment, no conditions, no second thoughts.

Here you touch the perfection of generosity. You give. You give an object to someone, and he or she receives it, yet it feels so natural, so in the moment, that it feels like nothing at all.

If you cannot look after yourself because you have no ethical
  discipline,
Then your intention to take care of others is simply a joke.
Observe ethical behavior without concern
For a conventional life—this is the practice of a bodhisattva.

IN 1995 AND 1996, BOTH GUERILLA AND GOVERNMENT
forces threatened the nine Cistercian monks at the monastery of
Notre-Dame de l'Atlas of Tibhirine in Algeria.

"Do we stay? Do we leave?" they asked each other. They knew
they were in danger and they each had a choice: return to France
or stay in Algeria.

They talked and they prayed, by themselves and together.

Each monk decided to continue the life that he had originally
chosen, a life of prayer, contemplation, service to the townspeople
and surrender to the will of God. None of them saw himself as living or dying for a cause. They did not see their decision as a way
to change the world. They simply followed their vocation, their
practice.

In the spring of 1996, seven of them were kidnapped and killed.

From a conventional point of view, their decision made no
sense. Their survival was threatened. They were not happy about
their situation and knew they were in danger. Nor was it clear
whether their decision to stay meant anything in the larger picture. For these monks, however, and for anyone who embarks on
the spiritual path, there is more to life than survival, happiness or
meaning.

Ethical discipline is first about how you choose to live your life, and, in particular, what you do when your survival is threatened, whether the threat is to your physical survival, or to your survival in a relationship, a job or a community.

What do you stand for? When do you take a stand? Sometimes it comes down to what you are willing to die for. This is not the practice of ethics as a way to improve your life. This is the practice of ethics as life itself.

Consider the question, "What am I willing to kill or die for?" *Kill* is included in this question because if you decide to die for something, you have already made the decision to kill.

Ethical discipline also means that you do not approach life in order to be happy or to resolve old emotional needs.

Consider a close friend, a person with whom you have a long and deep friendship. Do you see your friendship as a way to resolve old emotional needs? That is not usually why you treasure a friendship. You value the friendship itself, not what you gain from it or what it does for you. There is no calculation involved, and if there is, it is not a friendship, but a transaction.

In the same way, do not look to life for happiness, satisfaction or the fulfillment of emotional needs. Live life for life itself, whatever it brings you. This leads to another question. What about life do I love, and how do I live that love?

Ethical discipline leads you to a relationship with life that goes beyond meaning or purpose. These are abstract concepts, and they lead you to relate to life abstractly. You see yourself as an entity that exists independently of time and context. This is, of course, nonsense, but you are quickly seduced by the need to protect, maintain, refine or revise this identity and the reputation and legacy associated with it. The more concerned you are with purpose, meaning or identity, the less connection you have with life itself.

A third question, then, is, "What am I, apart from life?"

The ethical discipline you bring to your life is the expression of your connection with life. To paraphrase a Zen saying: "Deep connection, deep ethics. Little connection, little ethics. No connection, no ethics."

For bodhisattvas who want to be rich in virtue
A person who hurts you is a precious treasure.
Cultivate patience for everyone,
Without irritation or resentment—this is the practice of
    a bodhisattva.

HOW SERIOUS ARE YOU ABOUT WORKING THROUGH
your emotional reactions?

Are you like John of the Cross, the sixteenth century Spanish
mystic? After being tortured by the Inquisition, he was pardoned.
To redress the injuries done to him, albeit in a small way, he was
given a choice of monasteries in which to live. He chose a monastery whose abbot detested him. When asked why, he replied that
he wanted to deepen his practice of patience.

Are you like Atisha, the eleventh century Indian master? When
he came to Tibet, he included an especially obnoxious young boy
in his entourage, again, to be sure to have an opportunity to practice patience.

What about your roommate who never cleans up the mess he
made in the kitchen? Or the person beside you at work who is
always humming a song, and out of tune, too? Or the customer
service person who refuses quietly and calmly to help you with
your problem? Or the person who just backed into you and is
blaming you for the dent in his car?

It is hard to see these everyday irritations as opportunities, as
treasures.

When someone steps on your toes, literally or figuratively, you
feel a wave of reactive energy. It surges through your body—anger,
frustration, hurt, panic, resentment. You cannot tolerate it. If you

do not recognize this energy surge, it takes you over and pours out in angry words. Then you have a mess to clean up.

If you do recognize it, can you stay in the turmoil without expressing or suppressing it? Maybe you do not lose your temper, but you just quietly turn away and have nothing more to do with this person. Maybe you adopt an air of superiority, however subtle, and feel that you are taking the high road. These are still forms of suppression because the anger is still in your body.

Reactions are insidious.

You have to train and train. If you have to remember to practice patience in the moment, you have not trained enough, and you inevitably fall into some subtle form of expression or suppression. That is a lot better than spewing obscenities or bottling up your feelings, but it is not patience, not yet.

Like it or not, it is really helpful to have a person in your life who is a constant and annoying nuisance.

At first he irritates you. You do your best to persuade him to behave differently. When persuasion does not work, you try coercion. He is impervious. No matter what you say or do, it is clear he is not going to change. This nuisance is not going away. You have a choice, be constantly irritated or… Or what?

You grit your teeth as you realize that, if you want any peace, you are going to have to deal with your own reactions. What else can you do?

You start to pay attention to those reactions—the anger, the outrage and the feeling of being ignored. You become aware of how your body goes into knots and spasms every time you see or talk with him. You are obsessed with stories about what a horrible and inconsiderate person he is and what a noble and mistreated victim you are. Meanwhile, he is happily going about his day. You are the one suffering.

With no other option available, you pay more attention to what goes on in you. Since nothing else has worked, you decide to let him be and not try to change him, and to let your reactions be and not try to change them.

They surge, they clamor for attention, but you let them come and go. And they do come and go! They are not constant. That is the first bit of good news for you.

The second bit of good news is that you now have other options. You can, of course, continue to fight with your feelings, but you can also observe, explore or analyze them. Any of these may be helpful, though you usually fall into thinking very easily. More helpful is to open to them, look into them or receive and accept them. With these approaches, you are less likely to fall into thinking and more likely to discover through your own experience that you do not have to be run by your feelings.

How extraordinary! Through this nuisance you have discovered a dimension of freedom.

Now you train, so that that freedom is always available to you, first in easier, less demanding interactions, and then in more and more difficult ones.

The perfection of patience involves another step and a different quality of patience.

What is that stillness, that space, in which reactions arise and disappear? When you look at it, you see nothing at all. It is a bit frightening. It is like looking into the void of outer space. Something in you shrinks back.

This is the other level of patience, letting your reactions to that infinite nothingness come and go.

But do not stop there.

What are those reactions? Look deeply. They seem to be movement, but at the same time, nothing is moving.

Do not try to sort this out. Just rest and look, look and rest. Here, you find a different kind of freedom, a freedom that is both peace and clarity at the same time.

Listeners and solitary buddhas, working only for their
    own welfare,
Practice as if their heads were on fire.
To help all beings, pour your energy into practice:
It is the source of all abilities—this is the practice of
    a bodhisattva.

YOUR HAIR IS ON FIRE. YOUR HEAD IS BURNING. YOUR
only thought, your only concern, is to put the fire out as quickly as
possible. Is that how you approach practice, or do you come to it
grudgingly, resistant, kicking and screaming—only because you
feel there is no alternative?

Tokmé Zongpo is not suggesting that you approach practice in
a frenzy of fear and panic. He is talking about the quality and level
of energy you bring to it.

At first you think practice is going to make your life better. You
find that it does, but then your motivation begins to change. Perhaps you have a growing appreciation that you are going to die
and that there is nothing you can do about that. Perhaps you have
moments when your experience of life is so different that you realize that you are no longer content just to make improvements in
your life—you want to change your relationship with life itself.

Still, you are acting out of self-interest.

There is nothing wrong with that. You need a clear and strong
motivation to bring to practice the energy it requires.

Motivation becomes clearer and more energy becomes available when you are clear that you have no interest in conquering
the world, in being famous, in amassing wealth or power. You see
that riches, innovations, social movements, governments, philos-
ophies and fads all come and go. People fight about this and make

peace over that, but it is all the same stuff over and over again for hundreds, if not thousands, of years. You are done. You have had it with the world and you now look for some kind of inner peace or freedom.

Even more energy becomes available when you realize that all your old emotional needs are never going to be satisfied. They are ghosts from the past. You see there is no way to go back and make it all better. You accept who you are, for better or worse, and look to what is possible going forward.

And still more energy becomes available when you stop trying to live up to your own, or anyone else's, expectations of you.

You listen carefully to the teachings and your teacher. You figure out how the practices work. Then you go off on your own and practice. Survival, old emotional needs, identity—these concerns fall away. You put more and more energy into your practice, deepening your experience and understanding.

You are still taking care of yourself, albeit in a different way.

Now look at the mess of the world, the endless cycles of pain and joy, gain and loss, war and peace. You see how every person, not just you, struggles in his or her life—struggles and struggles and struggles. You are not alone.

At this point, a quite profound shift in your motivation takes place. Your practice is not just about you. You find yourself wanting, wishing or yearning to help others free themselves from their struggles, too.

Is this intention to free every being in the universe mere grandiosity, romantic idealism or a utopian vision of a perfect world?

It is none of these.

Your intention is just how it is for you—not that you can and will actually free all beings from their struggles, but that you want to, you intend to, and, even if the actual form of your life does not change, it is what you do in each and every interaction you have with others.

Take a moment, right now, and consider the idea of doing whatever you need to do to free all beings, everywhere, from their confusion, their emotional reactions, their projections, all their struggles with life. Time is of no consequence. A thousand years, a billion years, ten quadrillion years—it does not matter. Numbers do not intimidate you. A thousand worlds, a trillion worlds, each with billions of beings—it does not matter. You will do whatever it takes for as long as it takes. Take a few moments and feel what it is like to embrace that possibility.

To arrive at the perfection of energy, you have to take one more step. Ask yourself, "Who is it that helps beings?" and look, just look. As before, look and rest. Rest in the looking. Look in the resting. At some point, the conceptual mind drops away and you see that, while you help others in whatever way you can, there is no "you" there. Nor are there any "others."

Everything you do is simply a natural response to what you see, hear, feel and understand. You never think of another being, you never think of another soul, or a life, or a person. Those thoughts never cross your mind. You just do what life calls for, moment by moment.

Understanding that emotional reactions are dismantled
By insight supported by stillness,
Cultivate meditative stability that passes right by
The four formless states—this is the practice of a bodhisattva.

WHAT CAN YOU DO ABOUT ALL THAT STUFF IN YOUR head, the endless stream of thinking that jumps randomly from one train of thought to another?

Meditation practice seems to offer a way. You hear that you can quiet your mind by focusing attention on the breath or other suitable object (actual or imagined) or by learning how to let thoughts, feelings and sensations come and go on their own.

You focus attention on the breath, and that works as long as you are meditating. You observe feelings and sensations coming and going. They do not hook you, but you become increasingly aware of yourself as a watcher, a step removed.

When you go about your day, however, thoughts still intrude and distract. In the push and pull of daily life, you are usually lost in swirls of thought and feeling or you feel detached and disconnected, an observer, not a participant, in your own life.

Naturally you see thoughts and thinking as a problem and you wonder if you could stop thinking entirely.

You learn about deeper states of quiet, the four dhyanas (Pali: *jhanas*), for instance, and how to develop them. Your attention becomes more and more refined, more and more subtle, more and more powerful. You feel you have accomplished a lot, but emotional reactions still take over when you are not meditating.

In fact the only time you are the way you want to be is when you are meditating, in retreat, or in some other intensive practice environment. In the rest of your life, practice seems to make little difference in how you interact with others. You are thrown off by thoughts that come out of nowhere and by emotional reactions that take you unaware. You see again and again the same patterns of behavior in your life and you cannot understand the growing disparity between your meditation experience and the experience of everyday life.

Perhaps if you go further and still your mind even more, you could be free of thoughts and thinking completely? You rest in infinite space, utterly still and at peace. It is as if you have no body, but there is still a subtle sense of confinement and restriction. You rest more deeply, in infinite consciousness. The sense of restriction is gone, but you still do not feel free. You rest still more deeply. Now there is nothing at all, nothing, that is, except a vague sense of you. The stillness deepens, to the point that you cannot tell whether you perceive anything or not. The stillness and peace is extraordinary, but you do not see where it leads.

These four states are amazing experiences, all of them, but something is missing. Although you can still the mind to an extraordinary degree, when you try to live your life from that stillness or in that stillness, it does not work. As soon as you move, the stillness is gone. This is not what you expected and you do not know where to go now.

This approach to practice is a bit like learning how to paddle a kayak in a totally calm sea. As long as the sea is calm, you are fine, but as soon as there is a bit of chop or swell, let alone actual waves, you lose your balance and tip over. You can still your mind, but it is not much use in navigating the choppy seas of life.

When you are in a kayak, can you ignore waves breaking against your boat at odd angles? Can you ignore the swell that raises and lowers you five or ten feet? Of course not. As long as you see yourself as something separate from the ocean and try to keep still, waves knock you over. You are in the ocean! You are not separate from the movement of the ocean. When you understand that there is no way to keep yourself from moving with the ocean, you see that you have to be supple and flexible, you move with the ocean and constantly adjust your balance.

There is a difference between the freedom of a still mind and the freedom of no mind.

The freedom of a still mind is like kayaking in still water. It is peaceful. You can direct attention wherever you choose, and it rests there because you are so still. And it is almost useless in regular life.

The freedom of no mind is like kayaking with no fixed point inside you. You are not separate from what you experience. You are not watching it.

How do you do that? You look again and again at what cannot be seen, your own mind. Stillness does help with that looking. It helps a lot. Yet stillness by itself, even the extraordinary stillness of infinite space, infinite consciousness and so on, is not enough.

You have to see. And to see, you have to look.

Look again and again at what cannot be seen. At some point you see nothing—you really see nothing. You know, through your own experience, that there is no you in you, no fixed point, nothing. That experience makes all the difference. As thoughts, feelings and sensations arise in your life, you experience them without any fixed reference point. They are not "other." You move with them and through them, just like you move with and through the ocean waves in a kayak.

What do you do about thoughts, feelings and sensations? Nothing. They are free, completely free, to come and go on their own, just like the waves in the ocean.

So are you.

Why? Because you have lost your mind.

Without wisdom, the five perfections
Are not enough to attain full awakening.
Cultivate wisdom and skill
Free from the three domains—this is the practice of
    a bodhisattva.

WORDS, WORDS, WORDS. WORDS THAT SEEK TO MAKE
as precise as possible what cannot be put into words.

What is "full awakening?" What are "the three domains?" What
is "wisdom?"

Full awakening, or buddha, is the end of all confusion. Think
about that for a moment—the end of all confusion.

Three domains? They are the agent, the action and the object
of the action. For generosity, for example, the three domains are
the giver, the giving and the object given.

Wisdom is not a thing. It is intelligence, not in the IQ sense,
but the ability to differentiate what is from what is not. In other
words, you know that a thought is a thought, not a fact. You know
that a feeling is a feeling. Wisdom is not a conceptual intelligence.
It is a direct knowing, which is why it brings an end to confusion.

The first perfection, generosity, opens you to life. By itself, it
does not end confusion. You can give and give and give and still
feel separate from life because you are the giver giving something
to someone else. Thus, in addition to giving, look at who is giving.
You see nothing, of course, and that is the point. Rest in looking
at nothing. Do this again and again, whenever you give. One day,
something drops out. You see no giver—you see nothing. When
you give, there is no consciousness of "you" on your part. "You"

are not giving. It just happens, without thought, struggle or reaction. It is almost magical.

In the practice of ethics, you bring attention to every situation, consider carefully what is appropriate and do that to the best of your ability. This is a wonderful practice, but it is not freedom. It is not full awakening. To bring in the wisdom aspect, ask, "Who is acting ethically here?" As before, you see nothing. Again, you keep doing this. One day, you drop into empty clarity for a moment, and you just do what is appropriate, without thought, without all that careful thinking. Again, it is like magic.

For patience, you conscientiously check your every reaction, experience it and let it release. You can have the patience of Job and endure levels of hardship, privation, inconvenience and irritation that would drive anyone else insane. But patience alone is not enough. Again, ask, "Who is being patient?" Look again and again. One day, you are not patient at all, because nothing, not a single molecule in you, is irritated or struggling. The "you" that practices patience is not there at all.

It is the same with energy and stability in attention. Look at who is striving, who is meditating.

Bring the wisdom aspect into everything you do by looking again and again at who is acting, who is doing this, who is saying that. When you look, you see nothing. Keep looking at nothing, even as you go about the activities of your life.

At first you find this disorienting and a bit confusing. Then you become used to cutting the sense of self this way. There comes a moment when "you" drop away, maybe for a few seconds, a few minutes or a few hours, and you experience a freedom in life that you never expected. It is so simple! You cannot understand why you did not see this before.

All the old skills are there—generosity, ethics, patience, energy and stability in attention—but you no longer have to think about them. They just happen. Everything you know is immediately available, but not to you, because you are not there.

How do you do this? The same way that you get to Carnegie Hall: practice, practice, practice. First, practice to learn the skills. Then practice until they become second nature. Then practice until there is nothing left of you.

If you don't go into your own confusion,
You may be just a materialist in practitioner's clothing.
Constantly go into your own confusion
And put an end to it—this is the practice of a bodhisattva.

IT IS NOT ENOUGH TO LOOK LIKE A PRACTITIONER.
You may sit absolutely still in meditation, wear formal robes, perform rituals precisely and even teach and guide others. However, if
you are doing any of these to build skills and capacities that make
you more effective in your life, to enhance your status in the world
or to establish an identity, then you cannot say that you are practicing a path of awakening.

Why? Because you are using practice to improve the situation
of your life.

Suppose your boyfriend has broken up with you, your wife has
died or your child was killed in an accident. You struggle with the
loss and all the difficult feelings that come with it. If you try to
understand your suffering, you are soon lost in thinking. Instead,
each morning or whenever you practice, you rest in the experience
of breathing and open to everything in your body. You do this by
including the crown of your head and the soles of your feet in your
attention at the same time and let any sensations you experience
just be there, movements in a field of attention that embraces your
whole body.

At some point, you are able to feel clearly the pain of your loss.
This is grieving and it is important. The pain comes in waves,
sometimes triggered by a familiar object or a memory, sometimes

just on its own. The web of connection is unraveling, and that unraveling process is painful itself.

The pain of grief is not much fun. It feels devastating—as if you are being turned inside out. In the end, however, it is a sensation. The pain, in itself, will not hurt you or cause you any harm. As the web of connection unravels, you are gradually able to accept the loss and, bit by bit, you are able to go on in your life.

Now the hard part.

This is how you use meditation practice to work through difficult feelings. It is one way to use practice to improve the situation of your life. Granted, this is how many people approach practice, and it is how many teachers teach practice. A number of practice methods can be used to work through difficult feelings and difficult situations—mindfulness, of course, but also loving kindness, compassion, mind training, etc.

This is a utilitarian approach. It works, it is pragmatic, but it is essentially materialistic.

Do not use practice to improve the situation of your life. Use the situation of your life to practice.

When a relationship ends, use the pain and difficult feelings to deepen your practice, that is, your relationship with life itself. For instance, if you practice taking and sending, take in the pain and loss of others and give them your own happiness and joy, not to help you through the loss, but to deepen your intention to help others become free of suffering. When you look at what experiences loss, do so not to find relief, but to see vividly the infinite depth of being in the intensity of your broken heart.

Broadly speaking, there are two phases to the spiritual path: questing and resting. In questing, you are on a quest—awakening, enlightenment, peace, freedom, wisdom, God, a place you can call home, etc. You are not looking for a way to improve your life, to heal, to be successful or to satisfy any other conventional purpose.

One or more of those motivations may have started you on your way, but now all you have is your quest, and that leads you to study and train and practice. You are not aiming to improve your life. Rather, your life goes where your practice goes, and it is not always an improvement.

One day—it is impossible to say when or why—a shift takes place. In some way you have found what you are looking for. Your quest is over. You may not even recognize it at first—it can be more than a little confusing. You may be shocked, relieved, joyous or doubtful.

But your practice is not over. In fact, so many new possibilities open up that you now feel your practice is just beginning.

Practice changes at this point. It changes from questing to resting, to broadening and deepening your insight and understanding. Any aim you bring to practice is the reassertion of old patterns—the aim itself distorts experience. Instead, you see that you have to let all agendas go, every last one, even the idea of accomplishing anything. There really is nothing to achieve.

And that is what you practice. When your relationship breaks up, you practice, not to work through the loss, but to be awake and present in what life has brought to you.

A Zen master was heartbroken when her son died. At the funeral she cried and cried. Her disciples were surprised. "Didn't you teach us," they asked, "that everything is illusion?" She glared at them and said, "If you don't understand that each tear I shed saves countless sentient beings, you know nothing about Zen."

Are you a materialist in practitioner's clothing? It all boils down to one principle. Do you practice to improve the situation in your life, or do you use the situation of your life to practice?

You undermine yourself when you react emotionally and
Grumble about the imperfections of other bodhisattvas.
Of the imperfections of those who have entered the
    Great Way,
Don't say anything—this is the practice of a bodhisattva.

WHY DO YOU CRITICIZE OTHERS, PARTICULARLY THOSE
who, like you, are engaged in spiritual practice? What makes you
think you have a better understanding of their situation than they
do? What makes you think you could do better? Or are you just
jealous?

People start doubting you when you disparage those who are
regarded as very knowledgeable or capable. They see you as com-
petitive and mean-spirited when you demean your peers. When
you criticize those who are less knowledgeable and capable than
you, people wonder why you are not teaching or helping those you
are criticizing.

When you grumble about how this person is doing this wrong
and that person is doing that wrong, people soon stop listening
to you. They grow tired of you undermining the trust, friendship
or appreciation they have for those people, and they lose any trust
they had in you.

What do you gain here?

No matter how valid your criticism, you are a self-appointed
expert. You may not know it, but you are revealing to others how
arrogant and envious you are.

You hope to prove that you are intelligent, knowledgeable,
skilled, creative, strong, courageous or honest. Your criticism of
others demonstrates that you believe exactly the opposite.

When you are truly confident in your own knowledge, skill or creativity, you do not need to prove anything. You have no need to be critical and grumble about the imperfections of others. You can, instead, offer support, guidance and encouragement.

You may think you are holding yourself to a higher standard—not like those others! Yet the critical mind is devoid of joy, empathy or compassion. It is harsh and unremitting. The more deficient you feel, the more you criticize others. The more you criticize others, the more you reinforce the belief that you just do not measure up. It is a vicious cycle.

Just as people shrink away when you criticize others, parts of you recoil from the internal critic that is always telling the other parts of you what they are doing wrong. They shut down, and you lose connection with all the capabilities of those parts. How can you possibly be open, aware and respond creatively to the challenges in your life when you have an internal judge and critic constantly finding fault with the slightest deviation from the high standards it supposedly holds sacred.

When you ignore it, it talks louder and faster. When you shut it out, it uses your resistance as fuel for its criticism. The more you ignore it, the more vociferous it becomes. It keeps up a never-ending stream of critical commentary on your practice and everything you do in your life.

The belief that you are fundamentally deficient is a story—a deep-seated, self-referential and thoroughly convincing story perhaps, but a story nevertheless. It is a closed system that does not allow any questioning or any alternative understanding of your life.

Take a few moments and sit with this internal critic. Feel how harsh, how angry and how small-minded it is. Is this how you want to be?

Use any of the methods presented earlier to experience this part of you without being consumed by it—taking and sending, attention to the body, emotions and stories or open awareness. Keep opening to it until you are able to be present in it and aware at the same time. Underneath you find a deep-seated sense of deficiency, of not being enough, of not living up to certain standards. It feels as if you are fundamentally a loser, a fraud, a nobody.

Keep mixing your awareness with your experience of this story, this belief. At some point, a knowing arises—not an intellectual knowing, but a visceral shift in your body. You feel groundless and disoriented. You no longer know who you are. The usual references, including the impossibly high standards, are gone, and you experience a lightness and a joy you have never experienced before. It is as if you have stepped out of a dark cave into the sun. You take joy in the successes and efforts of others. From your own struggles you understand all too well how they can make mistakes or fall short of living up to the bodhisattva ideal, but you see them with understanding and compassion, not criticism. You no longer need to make yourself right at their expense.

This is not a trivial issue. The comparing mind does not let go easily. There are powerful sociological and cultural forces that keep it in place and reinforce it. Particularly when you are in a teaching position, or any position in which you are responsible for others, the comparing mind reasserts itself again and again. You are never the perfect teacher. You always fall short of your own ideals. You are acutely aware of your mistakes. There are always people that you cannot teach. But that does not mean that you are fundamentally flawed or deficient, though that part of you is often ready to jump up and grab the microphone.

When you feel the urge to criticize, keep your mouth shut. Feel what drives that urge. You are comparing yourself with others because that part of you feels "less than." Know that deficiency and know that it is a feeling, not a fact. Rest in that knowing and move into taking and sending—taking in the feeling of being deficient from others and giving them joy and freedom in return. The more you feel joy in others and in your life, the more you undermine the critical mechanism in yourself. Every time you touch viscerally the knowing that that mechanism is not a fact but a belief, you are set free, and the whole world is set free with you.

When you squabble with others about status and rewards,
You undermine learning, reflection and meditation.
Let go of any investment in your family circle
Or the circle of those who support you—this is the practice
    of a bodhisattva.

IMAGINE THAT YOU ARE GOING TO DIE IN A MINUTE.
Wherever you are when you read this, stop.

In one minute you are going to die.

One minute.

You have no time to call anyone, no time to settle your affairs
and no time to resolve any problems in your life. However you are
right now, wherever you are right now, this is it. You have one minute and then your life is over.

Tick, tick, tick, tick…

Done.

How did you spend the last minute of your life?

Were you concerned about status—at work, in your family or
with your friends? What about recognition, rewards or acknowl-
edgements? Did you think about what you owned, or how wealthy
or poor you are? Did you dwell on what others would think of you
after you were gone?

In all likelihood you grew quiet inside, very quiet. You looked
around, taking in everything you could see. You felt a bit in awe
at the prospect, wondering, perhaps, what the end of life is like.

Wealth, status, recognition and influence—these are what drive
you in your life. All of these, in one way or another, are driven by a

fear of death. Yet when you actually come face to face with death, these are the very things that fall away.

Look at your family dynamics. How much time and energy have you invested in being the family favorite, the golden child, the rebellious black sheep, the hapless loser or the pillar of the community? How much trouble and grief does this investment in your family circle bring you?

Look at your relationships with those who support you, those who provide you with an income, a job or a place in the world. You worry about what your boss thinks of you. You take even the most routine matters seriously. Your health goes to pieces under the constant stress of long hours and demanding assignments. You are courteous and cordial with your colleagues, yet you quietly enhance your own position behind their backs. Why do you seek more and more recognition, reward and responsibility? You are heavily invested in your circle of work, but what does it give you in the end?

In the light of death, you see clearly what is important and what is not. You are amazed at how much time and life energy you dissipate in matters that, in the end, do not mean much to you or do not make much difference in your life.

In the long run, wealth, status and influence are much less important than the moment-to-moment experience of life itself. Any form of idealism seems grandiose, arrogant and pretentious. When you face death, you open to what you have been closed to for much of your life. To deepen your relationship with life, focus on what is vital and important, and let go of what is incidental and peripheral.

Abusive language upsets others
And undermines the ethics of a bodhisattva.
Don't upset people or
Speak abusively—this is the practice of a bodhisattva.

A MAN CAME TO SEE A TEACHER AND ASKED TO BE
taken on as a student. The teacher looked at him carefully. Then
he said, "You are not ready. Come back in three years." The man
bowed and left.

One of the teacher's students asked his master, "Wasn't that a
bit harsh?"

"He really won't be ready for ten years," replied the teacher.
"To say that would have been harsh."

What is right speech? The traditional definition is speech that
is truthful, helpful, kind and timely.

What happens when you consciously try to say something in
a way that is truthful, helpful, kind and timely? You think about
what you are going to say, how you are going to say it, how it is
likely to be received and what you will say then. All that thinking drops you out of the conversation. You put on a performance
instead. You are so concerned about how you are going to sound
that what you say sounds affected and contrived, or you are completely tongue-tied.

Many people, even experienced practitioners, drop out of
awareness when they speak. They are not used to acting or speaking in attention.

When you open your mouth, habituated patterns often take over. How many times have you been clear about what you wanted to say and how you were going to say it, only to have it come out differently? In many situations you do not know which of the thousands of voices inside you has the microphone until you start to speak. You do not and cannot know what you are going to say until the words come out of your mouth.

When you speak, listen to the sound of your own voice—as if you were listening to another person. You may not like what you hear, but listen anyway.

If you hear an edge in your voice, you know that you are angry. If your voice sounds plaintive, you know that you are feeling weak or uncertain. You hear when you are selling your ideas or when you are trying to seduce someone against his or her will (there will be a little insistence or insincere charm in your voice). You may be surprised to hear yourself speaking in the voice of your mother or father and think, "That's strange. Where did that come from? That isn't me!"

In particular, when angry, abusive, sarcastic, undermining, condescending, accusatory, insulting, rude, offensive, pejorative, irrelevant or pointless words start pouring out, you hear it immediately and you stop.

You feel naked, open, and uncomfortable. Now you are back in the actual interaction. Look at the other person. Take in the situation. Open to everything that is going on, inside you and outside you. Then start again.

Do not confuse practice with result. The result is right speech—speech that is truthful, timely, easily heard and relevant. The practice is no distraction, no control, and no work.

No distraction means that you are present in the interaction, present with everything that is going on. You are not thinking about something else.

No control means that you do not think or strategize about what you are going to say or how you are going to say it. When you speak, what you say arises as a response to what you are experiencing with the other person, or you do not say anything at all.

As Rumi says:

A white flower grows in the stillness.
Let your tongue be that flower.

No work means that you are not trying to accomplish anything. For instance, if you are having a conversation with a friend or colleague and you think he is mistaken, instead of arguing with him, you respond to what he is saying and let him discover the problems, if any, in his thinking.

The result is right speech. What you say is true. You say it in a way that it can be heard. You avoid being unnecessarily harsh or hurtful. What you say is relevant—it applies to what is happening or being discussed.

Why is right speech so important? Most of your relationships with others involve speech. If you are not present and awake when you speak, you are not present and awake in those relationships.

When emotional reactions build up momentum, it is hard to
    make remedies work.
A present and aware person uses remedies as weapons
To crush craving and other emotional reactions
As soon as they arise—this is the practice of a bodhisattva.

CUT DOWN EMOTIONAL REACTIONS WITH THE AXE
of insight! Crush them with the force of attention! Annihilate
them with loving kindness! Flatten them with the steamroller of
emptiness!

Would it not be wonderful if you could actually do that—blast
emotional reactions to smithereens and be rid of them, once and
for all?

It does not work that way. When you attack them directly, they
disappear, adapt and return. Brute force is rarely effective.

You cannot kill emotional reactions. They are not alive. They
are not aware.

These lines are poetry, metaphor. Here the metaphor is war, a
common enough occurrence in medieval Buddhist cultures. Metaphors are useful because they cut through your intellect and touch
you directly. What is the message of this metaphor?

War is an utterly serious business. You fight for your life, the
well-being of those close to you, the world you want to live in. It
draws on all your resources, your energy, skills, attention, courage and determination. To be free of emotional reactions, you
also have to draw on all your energy, skill, attention, courage and
determination.

But metaphors are useful only up to a point. Here, the metaphor of war conveys the energy you need, but it does not convey

the subtleties of how to work effectively with your own reactive patterns.

These patterns are expert at survival or, to be more accurate, at persistence. They started as coping strategies that ensured your survival in difficult situations. They evolved into complex mechanisms that tenaciously react to any situation that poses a threat. They are programmed fighters.

Can you use your attention as a club and bash them into little pieces? Unlikely. Violence begets violence, and your patterns are better at it than you are. They formed in violent situations, situations that threatened your very existence. They have no compassion, no remorse and no awareness. They just run—ruthless, blind mechanisms triggered by any sense of threat or danger. They see the world in terms of the past and act accordingly.

They formed to protect you, but they have no awareness of who you are now or what your life is like. They are not active when you are present and aware, because attention and awareness inhibit their functioning. They spring up when your attention is elsewhere and when you are least expecting them.

When you oppose them directly, they chew up your remedies and absorb the energy of your efforts. They end up stronger than before, and you end up more reactive.

How, then, do you lay claim to your life and your human heritage without triggering the survival mechanisms embedded in these patterns? How do you draw on all your energy, skill, courage and determination?

Take an emotional reaction you know well—anger, pride, greed, guilt or any other. Pick one and let it come up. If you need to, recall or imagine a specific situation.

Feel how it takes expression in your body—a tightening here, a tension there, a weakness in the legs, a hollow feeling in the stomach. Do not focus on the sensations. Just open to them.

Make your whole body the field of attention and let the sensations associated with the emotional reaction arise in that field. Experience them as movements in the field.

Various sensations may catch your attention, and you fall into distraction. Sooner or later you recognize that you were distracted. As soon as you do, open again to your whole body, and let the sensations be there—like leaves swirling in the wind.

If the emotional reaction builds up momentum, it just runs. It consumes all your attention, and your attempts to change it become chaff in its gusts. However, you have other possibilities when you catch the reaction early—hence the need for attention and alertness.

Sometimes the emotional reaction releases as soon as you are aware of it, and there is nothing more to do.

Sometimes you cannot touch the pattern. It is just too hot, too full of fear. You are consumed by stories. You lose any sense of your body. You fall into distraction and confusion, but it does not last. The pattern plays itself out. You recover attention. And then you start again. You may fail a thousand times before you develop the skill and capacity to stay present in the reaction. That is why it is called practice. That is why you need to be determined. These are ghosts, usually from your past. They cannot harm you now, but to you, if definitely feels that your life is on the line, and that is where courage comes in.

At some point you experience the reaction physically and emotionally, relatively free of stories and associations. You experience long-held feelings that attention has never touched. It is often unpleasant, painful and frightening, yet a relief—all at the same time.

How, then, do you "crush" a reaction? You let it run inside you, experiencing it completely in a field of attention and awareness. It arises, churns you up with its turbulence, and then it is gone— one moment a terrifying ghost, then a gust of wind, then nothing.

In short, in everything you do,
Question how your mind is, moment by moment.
By being constantly present and aware
You bring about what helps others—this is the practice of
a bodhisattva.

BECAUSE TOKMÉ ZONGPO WROTE THESE VERSES AS reminders for himself, it is no surprise that he ends with a reminder that attention and awareness are everything.

The world does not unfold through thinking. It is the height of human arrogance to believe that the contents of your thoughts have any effect on the world or the universe. Mind is how you experience the world.

Only your actions have an effect.

You think you decide what to do. You think you act. You think you control your life, and, if you are strong or powerful or subtle enough, the lives of others. These are all myths.

What you do is not determined by what you think. Most of the time, what you do is determined by a pattern of reaction. Thinking, even the experience of deciding, is part of the pattern. It is often after the fact or peripheral to the action itself.

Thinking is always in service of one pattern or another. Frequently, it is the justification or explanation that the pattern presents to you after it has taken over your body, heart and mind and initiated action. Decision, in many cases, is simply an experience, a set of thoughts, feelings and sensations that accompany a course of action.

You think you decide what to do, but that is not the case.

When you encounter an unexpected situation—your girlfriend breaks up with you, a friend questions your integrity, you win the lottery—thoughts and stories swirl. You cannot even think straight. Hurt, shame, excitement or fear takes over. You gasp for breath. Your heart thumps. You shout and yell, frightening your girlfriend. Something shuts down in you, and you never speak to your friend again. You go on a spree and buy things that you never use.

Did you make any of those thoughts, feelings or physical reactions happen? What, exactly, did you decide here?

Consider a really trivial example: a crossword puzzle. You read the definition for one of the entries. You have a few letters as clues. You think of all the words it could be, but none of them fit. You are stymied. You take a break, make a cup of coffee, and suddenly, there it is in your mind, the word you were looking for.

Did you make that happen?

In today's world, the belief that you are the author of your life runs deep. When a situation does not go the way you expected or wanted, you look to see what went wrong and where you can lay blame. You look for an explanation that fits the belief that you are the author of your world.

If you really look at what goes on in your mind, you see that different kinds of thoughts, feelings and impulses are arising all the time. Some you act on. Some you do not. What decides? What leads one impulse and not another to become an action?

As soon as an emotional reaction is triggered, it shapes how you see the world. There is nothing you can do about that. Everything you do after that makes sense in the world projected by the reaction, even if it makes no sense in the world at large. Somewhere between ninety-eight and ninety-nine percent of your thoughts and feelings is stuff thrown up by one pattern or another. The only way to reduce the distorting effects of patterns is to bring as much attention as possible to what you are experiencing.

Thus, whatever you are doing, question what is arising in your mind. Do not believe any of it.

In complex situations many patterns are triggered simultaneously. Conflicting thoughts and ideas race around in your mind. Conflicting feelings tear your heart apart. Your body moves first in one direction, then another. Patterns and identities struggle to maintain themselves. It is their struggles that you experience as turmoil, uncertainty and indecision.

Absolute certainty and inflexible decisions are similarly generated. You cannot possibly think through what to do because all your thinking is in the service of one pattern.

In difficult situations, sit in the mess. Use the methods and practices described here to keep coming back to attention until you find a quality of open clarity—in the mess, not apart from it.

Clarity means that you experience what arises clearly. Thoughts and feelings arise like reflections in a mirror. When you look at a mirror, you do not see a mirror—you see reflections. When you know the reflections are reflections and not actual objects, you know you are looking at a mirror. Thoughts and feelings are similar. When you know that thoughts and feelings are thoughts and feelings, you know you are looking at your mind. That is clarity.

Open means you see without prejudice and without confusion. You do not suppress or ignore anything that arises, internally or externally. Regard all that you experience as a dream. At the same time, see what is what. Do not confuse one thing for another—experience every element in the dream vividly and distinctly.

The intensity of your thoughts and feelings lessens because you are in and aware of the space in which they arise. Like silence and sound or stillness and movement, thoughts and feelings are not separate from the open space of awareness. You still feel everything, but you are no longer struggling against it. It is tricky, because if you succumb to even a little distraction, you lose attention and you are once again lost in it all. Keep coming back to that open clarity and resting in the mess until you become aware of a timeless awareness that is you and not you. It is you, because you are aware. It is not you, because "you" as a separate entity is not there.

In that timeless awareness, a knowing arises. This knowing is non-conceptual. It is not driven by reaction or pattern. It arises from meeting, opening, understanding and accepting exactly and precisely what is arising in your life. You know where the imbalances are, not through thinking, but more through sensing directly. And you know what needs to be done to address those imbalances. That knowing takes expression through your body, through action.

That is how you bring about what helps others. Here compassion is a result, not a method. By not thinking about helping others, by not trying to be or do anything at all, you respond to the need of each moment, the direction of the present, the imbalances and pain of the world.

To dispel the suffering of beings without limit,
With wisdom freed from the three domains
Direct all the goodness generated by these efforts
To awakening—this is the practice of a bodhisattva.

DO NOT HOLD ONTO THE SMALLEST HOPE OR WISH
that you benefit from your practice. Let it all go—every last bit.

You feel good about what you have done. Yet to hold on to it
is to live in the past, not the present. Let it all go—even the good
that you do.

You may want to believe in the idea of goodness, that you can
dedicate it to the awakening of others, and that this kind of dedication also helps you in some way. Taken literally, these ideas
are fairy tales for children. Taken as they are intended, however,
they can move you deeply into the totality of experience, where
all words fail, yet you are able to respond to the pain of the world,
completely and unreservedly.

The bodhisattva path is a path of no reference, no reference at
all—not goodness, not awakening, not emptiness. Nothing. Your
actions come from the open clarity of awareness, not from your
thoughts and feelings.

Once again, take a moment and consider how your practice has
affected your life, how it has changed your life, perhaps. Or consider what you have learned or understood through reading these
notes.

Now, as the verse says, direct all that goodness to awakening.

Think of all beings, all the thousands, millions and billions
of beings in the world. Think about how they all struggle in their

lives, for food, water, shelter and security. Think of dedicating all the goodness you have generated in your life to their welfare. Do not hold on to the slightest bit for yourself. Everything, all of it, goes to them.

When you do this, you may feel a bit of a tug in your heart. Feel the tug, feel how you would like to hold onto a bit of the benefit for yourself, and, as you feel that tug, again, dedicate all your goodness to the welfare of all beings. Let it all go. Let it all go to them.

When the feeling of dedication is clear and strong in you, know that there are no other beings, there is nothing that can be dedicated and no dedication takes place. These are all just thoughts and ideas, ways you relate to what you are experiencing in each moment.

Rest right there.

In a sense, this is the same old, same old, but it is a pretty wonderful same old. Everything drops away, and there you are, awake and present, free from the three domains.

That is dedication in the practice of the bodhisattva path.

Following the teachings of the holy ones
On what is written in the sutras, tantras and commentaries,
I set out these thirty-seven practices of a bodhisattva
For those who intend to train in this path.

YOU HAVE COME TO THE END. IN YOUR HANDS YOU
have the essence of the bodhisattva path, set out by an intelligent
and devoted practitioner who lived in Tibet in the fourteenth century. It is a traditional path, a systematic sequence of practices
established by the Indian master Atisha in the eleventh century,
a sequence that became the model for the bodhisattva path in the
Buddhist traditions of Tibet.

In writing this poem, Tokmé Zongpo relied on traditional
teachings—the sutras, tantras, and commentaries—and, though
he does not say so explicitly, his own training and experience.

This path was his life. From his biography it is clear that he
did not seek fame, renown, riches or immortality. He took these
teachings to heart and lived them to the best of his abilities. He set
them down—for himself, of course, but for others, also.

An end is always a beginning.

What do you do now?

Because I have limited intelligence and little education,
These verses are not the kind of poetry that pleases
    the learned.
But because I relied on the teachings of the sutras and
    the revered,
I am confident that *The Practices of a Bodhisattva* is sound.

WRITING IS ALWAYS A CHALLENGE. PUT YOURSELF IN Tokmé Zongpo's position.

On the one hand, you have the example of those who have gone before you. Time, culture, politics and many other factors filter what you are able to study, learn and practice. You are exposed to only the very best of earlier masters, the very best that has been done, and you cannot imagine how anything you do or say or write could possibly compare.

On the other hand, you have what is happening in your own life. You know where you want to go in your practice, yet you feel a tension between what has come down to you from the old masters and what you feel you need to do to practice in the life you are living right now.

What do you do?

Drawing on what he had learned and what he had experienced in his own practice, Tokmé Zongpo wrote down these thirty-seven verses to help him focus his efforts.

You might consider doing something similar. You do not have to write thirty-seven verses, of course. You could write three or five or sixteen, or you could just start writing, and it ends when it ends.

What have you learned about practice? What reminders would you write for yourself?

However, because it is hard for a person like me with limited
    intelligence
To fathom the profundity of the great waves of the activity
    of bodhisattvas,
I ask the revered to tolerate any mistakes I have made,
Contradictions, non sequiturs, and such.

A LITTLE HUMILITY GOES A LONG WAY. YOU MAY BE
the most intelligent person in the room, or the most experienced,
or the most powerful, or the most… Still, there are always things
other people do better, points you miss, and depths you have not
plumbed.

Progress in practice is not linear. Sometimes it seems like
a series of stumbles from one understanding to another. After
months or years of effort, a single sentence or an unexpected
sound suddenly triggers a new insight or a profound opening. A
line or a verse that you thought you understood reveals hidden
dimensions. Your old understanding is not wrong. You now see it
as one facet of a multi-faceted jewel.

Thus, in composing these verses Tokmé Zongpo does not pre-
sume that he has plumbed the depths of traditional teachings or
has fully appreciated what others have done in the past. On the
contrary, he asks the masters of yore to be patient with him. This
is his understanding now. Tomorrow it may be different.

It is important to know what you know, and own it.

It is equally as important to know what you do not know, and
own that.

What do you do when you make a mistake? How do you
respond when someone offers you feedback? Or criticism?

Before you defend your position, your reputation, your view or your identity, listen to what others are saying.

Listen.

You may learn something, and it may be important.

If you have made a mistake, do not cover it up. Do not hide it. There is no need to be embarrassed. You are the only person who thought you might be perfect.

Mistakes give you the chance to learn something you did not know, and maybe did not know that you did not know.

A little humility goes a long way.

Through the goodness of this work may all beings,
In awakening to both what seems and is true,
Not rest in any limiting position—existence or peace:
May they become equal to Great Compassion.

YOU LIVE IN THE APPEARANCE OF THINGS AND YOU
take as true what only seems to be true. The challenge is to know
the difference between the container and its contents.

What you are cannot be put into words.

What can be put into words, what can be described, traded or
shared, is but the appearance of things, not what you are.

You need to know both the appearance of things and that there
is nothing beyond the appearance of things.

This is a mystery.

When you accept that mystery, you seek neither security nor
escape—the illusion of control on the one hand, the mirage of
transcendence on the other.

When you know that there is nothing but this experience called
life, there is nothing to do but embrace it in all its complexity and
simplicity, with all its joy and pain. When you understand why and
how everyone struggles in life, your only wish is that they find freedom, too, the freedom embodied by Avalokiteshvara, the freedom
of Great Compassion.

JUST AS A PLAY IS NOT SOLELY THE WORK OF A PLAY-wright, a book is not solely the work of an author. It would never have crossed my mind to write this book if a number of people had not saved the series of email newsletters that I began in the fall of 2010 and asked me to put them in book form. Encouraged by this interest, I began revising the initial commentaries in 2011 and completed the first draft of the manuscript in the spring of 2012.

In addition, Janaki Symon's incisive editing and constant encouragement helped me bring life and focus to the original draft. Comments from Ruth Gilbert and Jon Parmenter clarified a number of important points. Ann Braun, Rik Jespersen and Shawn Woodyard all offered helpful criticism. Christy Stebbins and Andy McLellan gave the text the final proofreading and offered many improvements. Finally, Valerie Brewster designed the book, giving it elegance and substance in all three editions—hardcover, paperback and digital.

My thanks and appreciation to all of you.

My thanks also to Diego Sobol and Majda Juric, Ann Braun and Claire Wheatley, and Jaynn and Harold Kushner, who all provided me with quiet and supportive environments in which I could work on the final drafts.

Ken McLeod

KEN MCLEOD IS KNOWN FOR HIS ABILITY TO EXPLAIN deep and subtle teachings in clear and simple language. "He distills the nature and purpose of Buddhism to make it accessible for any newcomer without dumbing it down," writes Phil Catalfo (*Yoga Journal*, July 2001) in his review of Ken's first book *Wake Up to Your Life*.

Born in England in 1948, Ken grew up in Canada and journeyed overland to India (in large part by bicycle) in 1969–70. There he met his principal teacher, Kalu Rinpoche. Ken served as his interpreter in India as well as during Kalu Rinpoche's first two teaching tours in North America. After Ken completed two three-year retreats, he was appointed to teach in Los Angeles. In 1990, Ken established Unfettered Mind, a place for people whose paths lie outside established centers and institutions.

In 1996, Ken roiled the Buddhist world with his model of one-on-one consultations on Buddhist practice. His approach is now regarded as a viable model for Buddhist teachers in the West. In addition to retreats and courses, Ken also conducted teacher training programs and mentored a number of newer teachers. He continues to do so on an informal basis.

In 1999, Ken established a consulting practice focusing on leadership skills, team building and personal and organizational effectiveness. He makes use of systems thinking to create organizational dynamics that naturally generate productive interactions within the organization. To this end, he has the ability to reformulate issues in such a way that his clients see for themselves how to resolve them.

Ken has a graduate degree in mathematics from the University of British Columbia (Canada), more than twenty years intensive training in Eastern disciplines (including Buddhism, tai chi and other martial arts), and over twenty years teaching and consulting experience.

NOTES

NOTES

CPSIA information can be obtained at www.ICGtesting.com
Printed in the USA
BVOW03s2148160316

440654BV00003B/86/P

9 780989 515313